# Interpreting the Universe

# INTERPRETING THE UNIVERSE

*by*

JOHN MACMURRAY

*Introduction by*

A. R. C. DUNCAN

HUMANITIES PRESS
NEW JERSEY

First published 1933; this edition first published 1936.

This edition reprinted 1996, with a new Introduction,
by Humanities Press International, Inc.,
Atlantic Highlands, New Jersey 07716

©1933 by Estate of John Macmurray
Introduction ©1996 by A. R. C. Duncan

**Library of Congress Cataloging-in-Publication Data**

Macmurray, John, 1891–
Interpreting the universe / by John
Macmurray ; introduction by
A. R. C. Duncan.
p. cm.
Originally published: London : Faber and Faber, 1936. With
new introd.
Includes index.
ISBN 0-391-03818-4 (pbk.)
1. Knowledge, Theory of. 2. Thought and thinking.
3. Whole and parts (Philosophy)  I. Title.
BD161.M23  1993
121—dc20                    93-20101
                              CIP

All rights reserved. No part of this publication
may be reproduced or transmitted, in any form or
by any means, without written permission
from the publisher.

Printed in the United States of America

# Contents

|  | Introduction<br>*A. R. C. Duncan* | vii |
|---|---|---|
| I. | THE UNIVERSE IN IMMEDIATE EXPERIENCE | 1 |
| II. | THOUGHT AS SYMBOLIC INTERPRETATION | 18 |
| III. | INTERPRETATION AND VERIFICATION | 35 |
| IV. | MATHEMATICAL THOUGHT AND MECHANISM | 47 |
| V. | BIOLOGICAL THOUGHT AND ORGANISM | 58 |
| VI. | PSYCHOLOGICAL THOUGHT AND PERSONALITY | 69 |
| VII. | LOGIC AND LIFE | 81 |
|  | Index | 93 |

# Introduction

## A. R. C. Duncan

Philosophical books published in the later part of the twentieth century are divisible into two very different types: those that overwhelm the reader with the number of pages required by the author in order to make his or her views clear and those that tend to be much shorter and challenge the reader to do some independent thinking. The first type are generally academic and discuss fairly fully a number of different and often competing philosophical issues in whatever may happen to be the prevailing philosophical jargon, while the second type are nonacademic and, though philosophical in nature and intention, are primarily addressed to the ordinary, thinking man or woman in the street. Martin Buber's *I and Thou* and Macmurray's *Interpreting the Universe*, to mention books by two very similarly minded authors, are definitely of the second type. Macmurray's book is written in a plain, clear, workmanlike style that avoids technical jargon as much as possible; it makes no attempt to survey the philosophical field, but raises and discusses a number of real problems that tend to arise when we set ourselves to thinking about the world in which we live or about the language we must use when doing so.

Because *Interpreting the Universe* is of this second type, I used it during the 1960s as an introductory textbook with a number of large first-year philosophy courses and continued to do so until the publisher was no longer able to supply us with sufficient

# INTRODUCTION

copies (we required at that time about 350 copies a year). This was a great disappointment both to me and to my students, as *Interpreting the Universe* was frequently described by students, year after year, as the most interesting book they had been required to read in their whole university career. This was a book that they wished to keep and reread. No second-hand copies ever appeared in the bookshops.

What, then, are the kinds of philosophical problems that turn up in real life? From his earliest days, Macmurray seems to have been aware that a very special problem arises in connection with the nature of persons. The universe in which we live obviously contains a vast number of different things or beings, but Macmurray, following a very old tradition, was accustomed to see the contents of the universe as falling into one of three different classes: inanimate things, living creatures, and human beings. Human beings were generally thought to be distinguished from inanimate things or living creatures by the possession of "reason," whose exact nature was variously described but whose possession was widely thought to be bound up with the powers of thought and speech. Since about the fifteenth century human beings came to be referred to as *persons*, the term Macmurray uses almost exclusively. A word of warning is in order here. In his early writings, including *Interpreting the Universe*, Macmurray frequently used the abstract noun *personality*, by which he meant that quality that makes a being a person; but, recognizing that the word had acquired a very different sense, he later abandoned it completely. As he explained in his Gifford Lectures,

> the term has been diverted from its natural meaning. We should expect it to refer to that quality or set of characteristics in virtue of which a person is a person; a property which therefore all persons share, and which distinguishes a person from all beings which are not personal. In fact it has been specialised to mean the quality or set of characteristics which distinguishes one person from another.

The problem Macmurray saw was that we have not yet come to

# INTRODUCTION

grips with the nature of the personal element in human experience; in plain terms, we have not yet learned how to think properly about persons. Macmurray's reason for making this somewhat astonishing statement is explained in *Interpreting the Universe*.

*Interpreting the Universe*

The first three chapters of this book outline a theory of knowledge that departs from the traditional pattern of such theories in several stimulating and fascinating respects. Macmurray invites the reader to consider the meaning and implications of some common but central terms in any attempt to think about knowledge. I shall make no attempt to summarize his clear exposition; rather, I will simply call attention to some outstanding points.

He begins with the concept of experience, which he divides under the two heads of "immediate experience" and "reflective experience." Immediate experience is a given unity of cognition, feeling, and active impulses. It contains a form of knowledge that is the presupposition of all thought. This is sometimes neglected by philosophers who start by considering scientific knowledge, which is the result of hard thinking. It is quite absurd to maintain that I do not know that the liquid in the kettle is boiling or that there is a thunderstorm raging outside, or to claim that I am misusing the word *knowledge* in making these simple claims. The scientific knowledge that I may acquire about the atomic structure of the material in the kettle or about the atmospheric conditions that bring about thunderstorms in one sense rests on the more simple claims. "*All thought presupposes knowledge*. It is not possible to think about something that you do not already know" (p. 6).

In the second chapter, Macmurray examines the nature of thinking, which he regards as a symbolic activity of the imagination. The activities of thought, which are brought into play by the awareness of a problem of some kind, are of two main types: on the one hand, description and analysis of the given in

# INTRODUCTION

experience, and on the other, acts of judgment and inference. He makes clear the distinction between images and words by what he calls the process of "reduction of imagery," or "abstraction." He points out that the act of supposing is integral to thinking, but, whereas we can suppose almost anything, profitable suppositions must be governed by the nature of reality. "What keeps the activity of the imagination within the limits of the necessary reference to reality is the retention throughout the process of thought of a structural basis which has itself been derived from reality by the process of analytic description" (p. 32). All thought must, therefore, be seen as having two aspects: a structural unity derived from the reality we are thinking about, and its material content. These structural unities are referred to by Macmurray as "unity-patterns of thought," as categories, or as logical forms.

In the third chapter, which concludes the exposition of his theory of knowledge, Macmurray discusses the nature of truth and various forms of error, warning against the dangers of overgeneralization and pointing out that in the scientific field the necessity of verification of all thought processes is completely recognized. Macmurray emphasizes that any process of thought that has any claim to be rational must submit to verification. No thought process can of itself guarantee the truth of its conclusion, but must be verified by being referred to reality as known in immediate experience that is not limited to sense perception but includes action. Certainty is not a characteristic of reflective knowledge; what we may expect, instead, is a continuous development in the rationality of our beliefs.[1]

In the second part of the book, chapters 4 to 7, Macmurray discusses the three basic unity patterns that he introduced in chapter 2: the mathematical unity pattern of mechanical

---

[1]. A fascinating application of this conclusion to the field of theological beliefs will be found at the end of Macmurray's early article "Christianity—Pagan or Scientific?" (*Hibbert Journal*, 1926).

## INTRODUCTION

thought, essential to thinking about inanimate matter; the biological unity pattern of organic thought, essential for thinking about forms of life; and the psychological unity pattern of personal thought. Both the mathematical and the biological unity patterns have been worked out in intellectual history, while the psychological unity pattern, Macmurray claims, still stands in need of being worked out. The mathematical unity pattern and its weaknesses are discussed in chapter 4 and the biological unity pattern and its weaknesses are discussed in chapter 5. Chapters 6 and 7 are devoted to explaining what Macmurray means by the psychological unity pattern and to giving a rough account of what it may be expected to contain. It was not until the Gifford Lectures in 1954, twenty years after the publication of this book, that Macmurray was prepared to offer a tentative formulation of the missing form of the personal, as he now called it. It is important to be aware that the adjective *psychological* may be used in two senses: either as meaning "pertaining to the science of psychology" or as meaning "pertaining to the human soul or self." Macmurray uses it mainly, but not exclusively, in the second sense. Of special interest in these later chapters are Macmurray's account of reason as "the capacity for objectivity," his descriptions of those who limit their rationality either to the material or organic modes, and above all, his constant emphasis on the point that "personality is mutual in its very being." "The basic fact about human beings, in virtue of which they are human, is that they know one another and live in that knowledge.... '*I*' exist only as one member of the '*you and I*'" (pp. 77–78).

The form of the personal, for which he was searching in these concluding chapters, is given in a (still) tentative form in *The Self as Agent*: The self must be represented as a positive that necessarily contains and is constituted by its own negative. This abstract formula is profusely illustrated through the two volumes of the Gifford Lectures, *The Self as Agent* and *Persons in Relation*.

# INTRODUCTION

*The Author*

John Macmurray (1891–1976) had a long and distinguished career as a professor of philosophy, mainly at the University of London (1929–1943) and then at the University of Edinburgh (1943–1957). He was a prolific writer and, after a few academic articles in the 1920s, he wrote books and articles aimed chiefly at the ordinary, thinking man or woman. His main interests in addition to philosophy were science, religion, and art. In philosophy his predominant interest lay in the nature of persons, which he saw as presenting the main philosophical problem of the twentieth century. Later, his preoccupation with the nature of action led him to advocate a revolution in philosophical thinking comparable to that undertaken by Kant. The common assumption that in knowing the mind had to conform to the nature of the object was abandoned by Kant, who tried instead to see what the consequences would be of assuming that the known object had to conform to the nature of the mind. Macmurray was brought up in the long tradition of Western civilization according to which the life of contemplation or pure thought was the happiest one could attain to, while the life of active participation in politics or business was a secondary matter; yet he eventually came to maintain that the capacity for action, which necessarily includes thought, was the distinguishing characteristic of human beings, and he defined reason as the capacity for objectivity. He argued that philosophers should learn to think from the standpoint of action, which involves participation in real life, instead of from the point of view of the pure thinking self, for whom the world is an object. Although this line of thought was to come after the publication of *Interpreting the Universe*, its foundations are laid in that book, which consequently is almost essential preliminary reading to the later Gifford Lectures.

In 1935 Macmurray published *Creative Society: A Study in the Relation of Christianity to Communism*, which arose out of the study of Marxist thought that he undertook in response to the question "What is Christianity?" Stylistically this book differs from

## INTRODUCTION

most of his other work in being written in a heavy Hegelian-Marxist manner. In it Macmurray distinguishes between belief in God and belief in belief in God, and also between pseudo-religion and real religion—necessary preliminaries to any serious study of religion, which he here identified with the human craving for a sense of community. In 1936, invited to give the Terry Lectures at Yale University (which were later published under the title *The Structure of Religious Experience*), he gave a much fuller and more satisfactory account of religion, claiming that the field of religion is that of personal relations and pointing to the similarities in the vocabulary of broken personal relations with religious language: fellowship, estrangement, guilt, forgiveness, reconciliation. Despite the brevity of this book, it contains Macmurray's most convincing and sincere exposition of his views both on the personal element in human experience and on religion.

In *The Boundaries of Science*, published in 1939 but originally given as the Deems Lectures at New York University in 1936, Macmurray expounded his views on the science of psychology and claimed that with the advent of scientific psychology the formal task of science was nearing completion. Any science is a form of human behavior, and psychology, the study of human behavior, is therefore committed to a study of itself. The concluding two chapters, "Psychotherapy" and "Fact, Motive, and Intention," are especially to be recommended.

In 1938 there appeared *The Clue to History*, which had been written several years earlier as a series of BBC lectures. After reading the text, the director of the BBC tried to get another speaker to give a more orthodox account to balance the series. No one could be found. After long delays, the Student Christian Movement Press undertook to publish the lectures. The book attempts to trace the rise of Christianity in the Roman Empire, during the Middle Ages, and in the modern world. In this book, Macmurray attacks the distorting influence that Greek philosophy, particularly its dualistic bias, has had on the formation of Christian belief, emphasizing that Jesus was no Greek

## INTRODUCTION

philosopher, but the last in a line of Hebrew prophets. He develops his doctrine of the three forms of apperception: the contemplative apperception of the Greeks, the pragmatic apperception of the Romans, and the essentially religious apperception of the Hebrews. Jesus is credited with the discovery of the personal and with forming the religious intention of expanding the boundaries of human community. It is perhaps Macmurray's most difficult book to read, but it contains novel and even startling perspectives on religious history and reality that will reward the effort demanded by its condensed style.

During the Second World War, Macmurray wrote no books, but published numbers of pamphlets dealing with various topical matters. In 1953–1954 he was invited to give the Gifford Lectures at his alma mater, the University of Glasgow. This provided him with the motive and stimulus to review the various strands of his philosophy and to expound it in a coherent whole. The lectures were published in two volumes, *The Self as Agent* (1957) and *Persons in Relation* (1961) (both republished by Humanities Press in 1991). In them he criticizes European philosophy since the time of Descartes as both egocentric and theoretic, and calls for the adoption of a revolutionary standpoint, that of thinking from the standpoint, not of the solitary self, but of an active agent partaking in the life of the world. Although he continued to publish until his death in 1976, the Gifford Lectures represent the crowning achievement of Macmurray's uncommonly prolific and highly original output.

Interpreting the Universe

## ONE

## The Universe in Immediate Experience

The study of philosophy is apt to resolve itself into an experience of progressive disillusionment. Ever since Socrates awoke to the vision of his own ignorance and proclaimed that at last he knew that he knew nothing, his successors have found themselves liable to the same humiliating discovery. They have found that the most painstaking endeavours to find the truth brought them no nearer to the knowledge which they set out to explore, and that all they had earned by their sleepless labour was the bedevilment of the certainties with which they started. It is the experienced philosopher, not the novice, who finds himself entangled in the question 'What is philosophy, and how does one set about it?'

The professional answers to this question are very varied and very difficult to reconcile. They give rise to controversies which are often bitter and passionate, perhaps because a philosopher's definition of philosophy must be something of an 'Apologia pro Vita Sua'. He is justifying his own asceticism before the tribunal of his own memory. But for all this the traditional common-sense of mankind in all ages and amongst all races persists in giving to philosophy a meaning which is both definite and constant, however difficult it may be to express. Everyone, even Macaulay's schoolboy, knows that philosophy is the search for wisdom rather than for a specific knowledge, and that it is a search which depends not merely upon logic, however necessary that may be. The

# THE UNIVERSE IN IMMEDIATE EXPERIENCE

philosopher should reveal himself not as a specialist in a particular field but rather as one who has grasped the significance of human life and achieved the ability, if not to live life well, at least to understand how it should be lived. This common-sense conception of philosophy probably comes as near the truth as any of the more meagre definitions which philosophers themselves have given. They, indeed, are driven to take shelter in modesty by the disillusionment of experience. The popular view has at least one great virtue. It makes philosophy significant and important, not a hobby of the intellectual who has not the courage to live, but an essential process in the development of life itself. From this point of view we can say that every man has his own philosophy, whether he can express it in the thin symbolism of abstract language or not. It forces us to realize that every period of human history is the embodiment of a philosophical idea, since the very activities and conventions which distinguish it from other periods are themselves the expression of one possible significance in which men may clothe their lives. It means, too, that there is a philosophy embodied in the contemporary world, if only we knew how to look for it and how to express it. If we could find it, it would interpret to us the meaning of our own history and so help to solve the critical problems which threaten to wreck our civilization.

It is all very well to say that every man and every society of men has its own philosophy. That is only true in a most unhelpful sense. It might be truer to say that their philosophy holds them in its grip and tosses them about helplessly from one surprise to another. The trouble is that very few men and fewer societies have any clear idea what their philosophy is. It remains unexpressed and half-conscious, implicit in their ways of behaviour, in their hopes and fears, in their ambitions and rivalry. The task of the philosopher is to turn the searchlight of deliberate thinking upon this heaving darkness. It is to express in coherent and meaningful terms what is usually only implicit in the way we live. It is this effort that draws the boundary line between practice and theory, between understanding life and living it. Nor can the

# THE UNIVERSE IN IMMEDIATE EXPERIENCE

effort to understand fail to make a difference in life itself. Even if it made not a particle of difference to what we do, it would still make the difference that we now do it with the understanding. Experience shows, however, that the difference can never be limited to this. When we understand, though not till then, we are in a position to control, to plan and to change.

The activity by which what is implicit in our behaviour is brought into consciousness and defined is the activity of reflection. When we reflect we are seeking to become fully conscious of something that is already present and felt to be present in our experience. We can only become conscious of what in this sense is already part of our activity by expressing it either to others or to ourselves. Our usual method of expression is language. An activity of reflection which does not involve the effort to express, in some form or other, what we reflect upon is impossible. Expression is an essential element in reflection. Now, that part of an activity of reflection which is specifically concerned with expression in words is what we call thinking. By thinking we succeed in giving expression to something which forms part of our experience, and so we bring it into full consciousness. When, through thought, we have achieved such an expression, we say that we understand what we were reflecting upon. Thus, nothing is understood until it is expressed, nothing can be expressed except through thinking, and thinking is the result of reflecting upon what is already present but unexpressed in our experience.

Philosophy, then, since it is one of the more elaborate and systematic forms of our reflection upon experience, involves a determined effort to become conscious of something that is implicit in the activities of human life and to express in words through thinking that on which our reflection is directed. The expression which we reach, and which in its completed form we call a system of philosophy, will be an understanding of our experience or at least of that aspect of our experience on which we have been reflecting. That is obviously not a sufficient definition of the business of philosophy, and we shall have to enlarge it in the sequel. But it will do to start with.

# THE UNIVERSE IN IMMEDIATE EXPERIENCE

Such a definition implies a distinction between our unexpressed experience and the expression of it through reflection. In some sense this distinction is an obvious and inevitable one. It is one thing to have an experience; it is another thing to express that experience. Even if expressing it is itself another experience that we have, it is at least an experience of a new kind and one which presupposes experience which is not expressed. Before we can express an experience we must have it, and having it is at least logically prior to its expression. We can be aware of things without understanding them. This distinction between expressed and unexpressed experience is itself very difficult, perhaps indeed impossible to define, because our understanding cannot but modify and amplify the experience which it puts into words. We have become accustomed in modern philosophy to use the term 'immediate experience' to indicate such unexpressed awareness. The attempt of philosophers to define what they mean by the term has given rise to a good deal of unsatisfactory argument. Such controversy must be fruitless. It is an attempt to express the inexpressible. To express in words that which is what it is because it is not expressed in words is to draw water in a sieve. To reflect on immediate experience involves the destruction of its immediacy. To think about it is to turn it into reflective experience. And any reflection upon it must be an effort not to portray it but to understand it. Immediate experience is by definition experience which has not been thought about. It is, therefore, a presupposition of our thinking, not something that can be an element *in* our thought. To insist on this provides no reason for holding, as some philosophers have done, that there can be no such thing as immediate experience. Thought is by no means the whole of experience. Consciousness has other functions and other capacities than reflection and expression. Life is not the same thing as talking. Action should not be confused with talking about action. If there were no such thing as action, there could be no discussion of it. There would be nothing to discuss. If there were no immediate experience there could be no reflection, because there would be nothing to reflect upon. The effort to deny the reality of

## THE UNIVERSE IN IMMEDIATE EXPERIENCE

immediate experience is, indeed, only the philosophical symptom of that disease which is apt to attack tired men and tired societies, a fear of life which shows itself in the substitution of pictures for realities, of symbol for substance, of the mimic warfare of words for the struggle of life itself. We cannot describe immediate experience because to describe it is to express and understand it. But we can understand why it is indescribable.

But though it must be impossible to describe the immediacy of experience it is quite possible to indicate, by means of examples, certain aspects of it. When I was a boy, I was very fond of skating and made persistent and often painful efforts to perfect my technique in the art. I remember, in particular, the complete failure of my early efforts to do the Dutch roll backwards. In these days I was a great believer in books and my failure drove me to the Public Library where I procured a book of instruction in figure-skating. I pored over it for hours until I felt certain that I understood perfectly how the feat was to be accomplished. When I returned to the ice I felt sure that I should have no difficulty at all. But I discovered that all my studiousness had made precisely no difference. While I performed my clumsy antics, an expert who had been watching my efforts came up and talked to me sympathetically. 'What you want', he said, 'is just to get the feel of it.' He took me by the arms and proceeded to swing me through the movements. The effect was immediate. In a few seconds I had got the feel of it and all my difficulties vanished as if by magic. That simple experience is a good example of the distinction which we are discussing. 'Getting the feel of it' meant simply 'becoming aware of it in immediate experience'. It was something totally distinct from understanding it as expressed in terms of thought and description. It is possible to understand the expression of an experience without having had the experience, and even to find that such an understanding helps very little towards having it. Yet the expression of it and the understanding that results could obviously never have arisen at all unless someone had first had the experience immediately.

The importance of this distinction can best be seen if we

# THE UNIVERSE IN IMMEDIATE EXPERIENCE

formulate it as a general principle. *All thought presupposes knowledge.* It is not possible to think about something that you do not already know. It may be true that some things that we know cannot be understood or even described. But it is certain that nothing that is unknown can be described or understood. This is a principle which is frequently overlooked in philosophical discussion. We construct theories of knowledge which imply that knowledge is the result of thinking, and that it is, therefore, essentially bound up with the processes of reflective activity. The simple observation that you must know something before you can think about it completely upsets the equilibrium of all such theories. It is because we know things and are interested in them that we think about them at all. And the reason why we think about them cannot be in order to know them but at the most in order to know them better. The probable reason why the simplicity of this fact has often been overlooked is that our modern philosophy has been very largely concerned with the development of science. Scientific knowledge is, of course, the result of systematic activity of a reflective kind. In our concentration upon this we erect science into the type of all knowledge. We forget, in our preoccupation, that the kind of knowledge that science achieves is the result of investigating a world that we already know. The conclusions of some centuries of scientific research into the characteristics of matter constitute only a minute portion of our knowledge of the physical world. Men knew the world they lived in long before science was thought of. And in some ways, perhaps, they knew it better and more intimately than most of us know it to-day, since we took to living in towns and travelling in motor cars. That immediate knowledge of the world which is the effortless result of living in it and working with it and struggling against it has a much higher claim to be taken as the type of human knowledge than anything that science either has or can make possible. For the scientist takes this immediate knowledge of the world for granted and bases himself squarely upon it by his continuous appeal to facts. His particular business is simply to interpret it, to express it in such a way that we understand what

# THE UNIVERSE IN IMMEDIATE EXPERIENCE

we already knew in a quite different and immediate fashion. The understanding of the world which we gain through science can never be a substitute for the experience of it that we have in the normal unreflective process of living. Apart from this experience, indeed, all scientific conclusions would be completely meaningless, with no significance of any kind. They signify something only because they interpret our immediate knowledge of the world. If we did not know what water is by drinking it and washing in it and boiling it in our kettles, the scientific statement that water is $H_2O$ would be merely a meaningless noise. Yet time after time, in discussions of science and its discoveries, we find people talking as if the discoveries of science wiped out our unscientific knowledge of the world and put something quite different in its place.

Knowledge, then, is first and foremost that immediate experience of things which is prior to all expression and understanding. Upon this primary knowledge all reflection and all thought are based. This perhaps is specially obvious in our knowledge of people. When I say that I know my father, the knowledge I am speaking of has nothing to do with the results of my thinking about him, nor has anyone any doubt of what I mean. But if I tried to describe my father to someone who did not know him I should find it a very difficult task. I should have to reflect and think and express the results of my reflection in words. Probably the result would seem adequate neither to the listener nor to myself. And if later the person to whom I tried to express my knowledge made the acquaintance of my father he might very well tell me that I had given him a quite false description. He might even say that it was obvious that I didn't understand my father. But he would never dream of denying that I knew him. It is one thing to know a man and quite a different thing to write his biography. The same is clearly true of other things. If I ask a Londoner whether he knows St. Paul's Cathedral, he will almost certainly answer 'Yes'. But that would not imply that he could put his knowledge into words, that he could describe the Cathedral in any adequate way to someone who has never seen it. Still

# THE UNIVERSE IN IMMEDIATE EXPERIENCE

less would it imply that he could give an accurate account of its architecture, of its decoration, of its services or of its history. It is quite possible that he has never thought about St. Paul's Cathedral at all, though he knows it quite well. If he did begin to think about it, to study it carefully, to read books about its structure and its history, he might come to know it better, though even that is by no means certain. Reflection may raise our knowledge of the world to a higher power. It can do no more than that. However far it carries us, we must always presuppose and depend upon the immediate unreflective knowledge which is the foundation of everything else.

It is necessary at this point to guard against a misunderstanding which is both insidious and prevalent. Immediate experience is not the same thing as elementary or primitive experience. It has its own growth and its own stages of development. It is not something that belongs to our childhood and from which we gradually depart, neither is it an unchangeable substratum which accompanies us and all men throughout life. It is different for different people. It grows richer with the growth of experience. It is clarified and reorganized by the thought and reflection which is based upon it. It has all the capacity for growth and development, for differentiation and integration, which belongs to life itself. The processes of reflective thought as well as the reflective experiences of the artist or the mystic are bathed in it. They are born and die in it, dissolving once again into the soil from which they sprang and enriching it with a new fertility. If this were not so, no amount of effort and practice could ever increase by a hair's breadth our capacity to live in the world. We could not learn to walk or to speak, far less to develop the delicate skill that is requisite for all the characteristic activities of human life. This fact is obscured for us through the development of reflection itself. The tendency to think and the even simpler tendency to speak about what we experience is so early developed in us and becomes such an integral part of our consciousness, that it is hardly possible to be aware of anything or to engage in any activity without an element of reflection entering in. But this does not

# THE UNIVERSE IN IMMEDIATE EXPERIENCE

alter the fact that immediate experience and reflective experience are different in kind, and that in important respects their development is different and unrelated. We may develop thought to a point at which it becomes the enemy of immediate experience and begins to destroy our capacity for spontaneous activity altogether. One still finds people who possess a peculiarly rich knowledge which has developed unconsciously through a long, vivid and varied experience of life and in whom the capacity for reflection has remained untrained and undeveloped, in whom even the capacity for speech or expression has remained meagre and difficult. These, of course, are exceptional cases, but they draw attention all the more vividly to the distinction we have to make. In the normal case the present range and depth and character of our immediate experience is largely determined by past reflection upon the things we know. The artist sees differences in colour that are indistinguishable to other men. Immediate experience is not, therefore, primitive, raw experience, unaffected by thinking, nor is thinking the only instrument which we possess for the enrichment of our capacity to experience. The immediacy of an experience consists simply in the fact that we are immersed in it, that we are living it, and not setting ourselves over against it, as something other than us which we can contemplate and study. We are not asking questions about it and trying to give answers.

Immediate experience, therefore, is not the same at all times. It is different for different persons. It varies with their age, temperament and training, with the situation of the moment and with the tradition and habit of the society in which they live. It is simply every experience and all experience in so far as it is unreflective. It is experience lived through, not thought about. We cannot, therefore, give an account of its immediacy. We can, however, indicate the main contrast between immediate experience and the expression of it through which it is interpreted in reflection. In contrast with reflective experience, its essential character is its unity and completeness. Nothing in it is really separate from anything else. Its parts are not 'cut off with a hatchet'; they flow

# THE UNIVERSE IN IMMEDIATE EXPERIENCE

into one another and belong together. Its aspect as knowledge, for instance, is not a separable part of it. It is unified with and coextensive with feeling and action. It is our consciousness in living rather than our consciousness of living. In immediate experience we know anything by being interested in it, by desiring it, by loving or hating it, and above all, by doing things with it. The knowledge that we show in playing a game of tennis is part of the activity of playing it. It is not separable either from the playing or from the pleasure in playing which pervades it. These basic aspects of experience—cognition, conation and feeling—are fused into a single whole in the living experience.

Now contrast this with reflective activity. The moment we reflect upon what we are doing, we stand back from life and assume the attitude of spectators. We stop living and begin to think. A division appears between us and what we are thinking about. The unity and wholeness of living experience is broken. We begin to engage in an activity of thinking which is separate from and contrasted with the other aspects of our conscious life. When we are thinking we are not acting, we have postponed action for the time being. If we are asked then what we are doing, we are wont to reply that we are doing nothing, just thinking. Feeling is not necessarily suppressed even if action is. Indeed, there is a reflective experience in which feeling is the activity upon which we are concentrated. But if it is understanding which we are after, and concentration is necessary, feeling, too, will be suppressed, and the whole of our activity will become an activity of cognition. By contrast with immediate experience, therefore, reflective experience is abstract, incomplete and relative. It is abstract because it is separated off from the unity of immediate life and becomes a partial and one-sided expression of our capacity as persons. It is an activity of cognition merely, torn from its setting and separated for the moment from the other aspects of our personality. It involves a concentration of energy and attention on one aspect of experience and an exclusion of the others. This, in turn, involves us in a sense of incompleteness. Thought is always seeking to get further, to think itself, as it were, beyond

# THE UNIVERSE IN IMMEDIATE EXPERIENCE

thought, to become a satisfactory substitute for feeling and action. That is, in the nature of things, impossible. Thought can only complete itself when we cease to think, and turn to the other essential aspects of our experience which thought excludes. The same characteristic shows itself in the sense of relativity which pervades thinking. So long as we remain within the activity of reflective thought, everything that we think refers beyond itself. This reference of ideas to reality is the most persistent problem of the theory of knowledge. It expresses the fact that thought is not and cannot be self-contained and absolute, but must pass over for its completion, and to reach the concreteness of reality, to something which is not thought but existence. Thought which seeks to complete itself within thought merely involves itself in antinomies, in contradictions which cannot be avoided because they arise from the abstraction by which thought is constituted. Thought which seeks completeness in itself is trying to be life instead of an aspect of life. It is the frog trying to blow itself out to equality with the ox, pretending that the part can absorb the whole. Thought is mental activity only, and as common sense tells us, mental activity is not real activity. We cannot escape from the contrast between thinking and acting. We cannot help recognizing that when we are only thinking we are doing nothing. It is this effort to make thought a substitute for action, independent of action for its completion, that constitutes intellectualism. Intellectualism is the neurosis which results from the desire to escape from the necessity of action by spinning out thought to infinity.

We must now consider the special characteristics of philosophical reflection. The different divisions of reflective thought are determined primarily by the object upon which reflection is directed. The different sciences, for instance, are primarily differentiated by their subject-matter. Philosophy is in the same case. What distinguishes it from other forms of reflection is that it is directed upon experience as a whole. It is concerned to express and interpret the universe, not a part or an aspect of the universe. To ask, as one may be inclined to do at this point, whether the

## THE UNIVERSE IN IMMEDIATE EXPERIENCE

universe is a whole, and whether, therefore, there is anything for philosophy to reflect upon, would be to misunderstand the issue. The universe as a whole does not mean the aggregate or totality of all that is in it. This, indeed, is a contradictory conception, since the universe is infinite and cannot be a totality. By the universe as a whole, one means the universe in that quality of completeness and wholeness which is given in immediate experience, the absence of limits and clear-cut boundaries, the *qualitative infinity* which characterizes it in all its parts. It is this very wholeness and completeness which belongs to immediate experience always, and which is always absent from reflective experience, that philosophy reflects upon and seeks to explain. This becomes clearer when we contrast philosophical with scientific thought. Science and philosophy are both reflective activities and, therefore, they are both abstract and partial activities. But science is abstract and partial in a way that philosophy is not. For science always thinks about a part of what there is to reflect upon, never about the whole. It limits itself to a particular subject-matter. Indeed, there is no such thing as science, but only a number of different sciences each dealing with a part of what is given in immediate experience. Philosophy is not abstract or partial in this sense. There are not different philosophies as there are different sciences. There are merely different attempts, more or less successful, to create philosophy.

The characteristic of immediate experience is that it is given in actual living as a whole, and this whole is broken by reflection. The partiality of all reflection is discovered everywhere within the field of reflection, and so raises the problem of overcoming within itself the imperfection that attends upon it. To this task philosophy addresses itself. It becomes the effort to express, or rather to reproduce in reflective expression, the wholeness of experience which has been lost. Consequently, it depends upon and presupposes that knowledge of the wholeness of experience which is given in immediate experience itself. The philosopher does not need to prove that reality is a whole, though he sometimes tries to do so. Indeed, it cannot be proved. But that is because, unless it

# THE UNIVERSE IN IMMEDIATE EXPERIENCE

were already known, unless it were given in immediate experience, philosophy itself would never arise. This is merely to repeat, in a particular context, that all reflection is an effort to express what is already known.

It must be impossible to describe this wholeness in immediate experience by reproducing it in reflection. To describe it we should have to analyse it and so to break the wholeness. But it is possible to indicate certain aspects, to point to certain features of our experience which remind us of its wholeness as we live it. There is one distinction which we cannot avoid in any attempt to do this, the distinction between ourselves and what we experience. Even here we can remind ourselves that in unreflective living the distinction between ourselves and what is not ourselves is not present. We live as part of the whole of things, without contrasting ourselves with the rest. It is only when we reflect that the consciousness of being set over against the world, of standing apart from it in isolation, makes its appearance. And one of the major problems that faces the philosopher is the paradox that in thinking about the world he is at once setting himself over against it, and recognizing that he is part of it. One aspect of the effort to express the wholeness of immediate experience is, therefore, the effort to express the unity of the self that thinks with the world which is the object of its thought.

But if for purposes of indicating the wholeness of immediate experience we make this distinction, we may notice first the wholeness of the self in immediate experience. When I am living, and not reflecting upon life, I am myself as a whole. The whole of myself goes into my activity, whatever it may be, and all the time. Action and feeling and apprehension are fused inextricably in one. I do not think first and then act. My knowing is part of my action, or rather an aspect of it, and the whole is shot through with feeling. The action and the consciousness in the action have an emotional tone which varies as they vary, but always remains one with them. This is what I mean by the wholeness or completeness of the self in immediate experience. Every aspect of my selfhood is combined and unified in every activity.

# THE UNIVERSE IN IMMEDIATE EXPERIENCE

Similarly, what is experienced has a wholeness which is absent from the object of reflection. In immediate experience the world as well as the self is one—an unbroken unity and continuity of being. The passage of time from one moment to the next is given as a wholeness or continuity. There is no problem of joining together separate moments—the problem which faces reflective thought when it seeks to express the nature of time. Time is, in fact, given in immediate experience as an infinite whole, and what reflection calls its infinity is nothing but the absence of any limits in our experience of it. Past and future are, as it were, gathered up in the present rather than distinguished from the present in the immediate experience of living. Space, too, is given as an infinite whole, as the roominess of the world in which we are acting, a roominess which has no boundaries but which is the experienced possibility of going outwards from where I stand in all directions. That is why we find in philosophical reflection that space is so paradoxical. The whole of it seems to be given in any part of it. Between any two points, however close, there is an infinite number of other points. In this given unity of space-time objects appear and disappear and change their characters. Attention singles one out but does not separate it from the rest. When I look at a particular object that is clearly defined against a background of other objects less and less clearly defined as we go out from the centre of attention, it is experienced as part of the whole within which it is selected. When I turn my eyes to a second object, that, in turn, stands out more clearly, while the first slips quietly away into the background from which it emerged. These things indicate that the objects which thought carves out and isolates in separate words are given originally in immediate experience as inseparably one, as merely so many different definitions and differentiations of a limitless matrix. They are in the world and the world is in them.

There is one important corollary of this view of immediate experience which deserves special attention. Immediate experience cannot be equated with sense-perception. The cognitional aspect of immediate experience is, no doubt, in the main percep-

# THE UNIVERSE IN IMMEDIATE EXPERIENCE

tual, though it also involves imagination. Still less can it be equated with visual perception of the external world. No partial experience in which one element or one capacity of personal consciousness is singled out can be immediate. Sense-perception is itself an abstract conception, and represents an ideal limit or zero of cognitional consciousness at which awareness remains, practical activity has ceased and no reflective activity has begun. Such a conception, however useful it may be for purposes of analysis, can represent no real experience. For whatever else is present in an experience, activity must be. When practical activity ceases, it must be continued in some reflective activity, or consciousness will disappear altogether. When we stop acting and look at things the result is not sense-perception but the beginning of reflective activity of an æsthetic character confined largely to the visual field. Much fallacious theory seems to me to arise from confusing this reflective visual activity with immediate experience. The cessation of practical activity destroys the immediacy of experience. If, however, we turn our attention to the perceptual aspect of immediate experience, we discover another example of the unity which is broken by reflection. We find a fusion of perception and imagination. This shows itself, in the first place, in the difficulty of distinguishing image and percept in terms of their inherent characters. Under psychological analysis, as Hume pointed out so clearly, percept and image are resolved into the same ultimate elements, what are nowadays called sense-data or sensations. The characters by which we normally distinguish between perception and imagination are accidental. If I see something with my eyes closed I know that it is an image. If I saw the same image with my eyes open I might, under exceptional circumstances, take it for a real object. When that happens it is called hallucination. The fact that hallucinations can occur, however rare they may be, shows that there is no inherent difference between the image and the percept. We may notice, in the second place, that the objects of imagination emerge from their background and fade back into it precisely as do the objects of perception. They are changing characters of a whole which is in

## THE UNIVERSE IN IMMEDIATE EXPERIENCE

them and which they are. This background in its completely undifferentiated character is space-time, and the space-time matrix in which these images are born and into which they fade again is the same space-time in which the objects of perception appear, change and disappear. That is itself a matter of immediate experience. You have only to look at the world in front of you and then close your eyes to realize it. The space that you see with your eyes open remains when you close your eyes as the background of all the images that begin to appear.

It is this wholeness and completeness of immediate experience which we express when we speak of 'the infinite'. The term is, of course, a negative term, because it is the reflective expression of something which cannot be given in reflection. The thing itself is more positive than anything else we know. It is in a special sense 'the real'. It is simply that something which is one and the same in all immediate experience, which includes it all, in which all determination and difference appears and to which everything belongs. It is only through the inadequacy of reflection that the infinite seems to lie beyond everything that we can think or do, so that it seems to be the result of adding more and more until we are breathless with the effort. The infinite is the universe in immediate experience. It is given always and everywhere in the finite. As space, for example, the infinite is given in any geometrical figure. Spinoza made this clear once and for all. Even to our vision a triangle appears as a limitation of that which is beyond all limits. In apprehending the finiteness of the triangle we apprehend with our eyes equally the infinity of space.

Philosophy, then, is the attempt to express the infinite in immediate experience through reflection. It would be equally correct to say that it is the attempt to express reality. For reality is essentially the concrete wholeness which characterizes immediate experience. Whatever is abstract, whatever is isolated and separated out from the infinite in which it has its being, becomes to that extent unreal. This, I think, is what Spinoza means when he talks of the unreality of the finite in so far as it is finite. To isolate anything from the whole in which it has its being is to destroy its

16

# THE UNIVERSE IN IMMEDIATE EXPERIENCE

reality by depriving it of the possibility of completeness. It becomes essentially incomplete and meaningless when torn from its setting. Reality, therefore, is bound up with the unity and completeness of the world in our immediate experience of it. When any element in that experience is isolated by the processes of reflection, it becomes an idea, no longer a real thing; and every idea clamours to be referred to reality, to be replaced in the concrete world of existence from which it was derived. Ideas are unreal just because they are ideas, abstract and isolated. To add idea to idea, to organize ideas in systems and to expand these systems without end, brings us no nearer to reality. To reach reality we must overcome the abstraction of reflection itself.

Philosophy, then, is concerned to express infinity or reality. It is reflection in search of an understanding of the wholeness of immediate experience, not of partial and isolated aspects of it. It is reflection upon the universe in immediate experience, upon that infinite 'One and the Same' which is always present in any experience of ours that is immediate, alive and concrete. Knowledge, in the primary sense—in the sense in which it is presupposed in all reflection, and forms the necessary foundation for all thought—is the cognitive aspect of this living unity. Such knowledge, however, is not reflective knowledge, and philosophy is reflection. It is constituted by our effort to reflect upon the wholeness which is immediately given in that primary knowledge and to give expression to it through thinking. It is the effort to represent reality in words.

## TWO

# Thought as Symbolic Interpretation

The first question that faces us, when we turn our attention to the efforts of deliberate reflection, is the question of how thought arises. For reflection is certainly not a primary and self-explanatory state of consciousness. Immediate consciousness, we have seen, is a complete and unified activity of living in which cognition is an aspect, not a separate part. Before any deliberate thinking can take place something must happen which breaks the unity of life and concentrates our energy upon one abstracted element in the whole. Life is essentially concrete activity. Thought involves the temporary suspension of concrete activity. It holds up the action of life. We *stop* and think. What is it, then, that brings about this stoppage of the normal processes of life-activity? What, in other words, is the general reason, or rather the general cause, of reflection?

The primary cause is some recognized failure in concrete activity. We stop to think because our undeliberate action has gone wrong, or because the immediate motives which normally determine the direction of action have failed. Suppose, for instance, that in walking from one village to another along a road with which we are unfamiliar we come to a fork in the road with no indication whether we should go to the left or to the right. We have been following the road which led to our destination. Suddenly it has become two roads and we are physically incapable of following them both at once. We are brought to a standstill. Our

# THOUGHT AS SYMBOLIC INTERPRETATION

immediate experience provides no motive which will select one rather than the other. We are compelled to stop walking and to reflect.

There are many other ways, of course, in which the stoppage of action can be brought about. But all of them are in the nature of breakdowns in the primary processes of spontaneous activity; and all of them give rise to the state of mind in which thought begins, a state of hesitation. Thought begins in doubt. It is only when either artificially or naturally we are in two minds, when we are faced with a question to which there may be two answers, that reflection becomes possible. This state of doubt, with the questions in which it formulates itself, arises always, directly or indirectly, from some hitch in the process of living, or rather from the consciousness of such a hitch. This consciousness involves both a feeling of dissatisfaction and the recognition of an unsatisfactory situation.

Such an account of the origin of reflection implies also a recognition of the end or function of reflection. Its function is to overcome the cessation of action which has occasioned it, and so to enable us to resume the concrete activity of life which has been interrupted. The business of thought is to answer the question and to resolve the doubt which lies at its roots. This is the only possible account of real thinking. There are, of course, types of thinking which are pathological or diseased, in which the process of reflection, once started, refuses to come to an end; in which even the desire to reach a real solution has failed and thought is carried on for its own sake. Such thought, in my opinion, is definitely abnormal and irrational, however logical it may be. However much rationality there may be in it, there is no reason for it. It demands to be explained, as all abnormality does, by reference to the normal, as a distrubance of the natural process of personal life. Real or normal thinking is, as we have seen, a natural interruption of the process of living, and its justification can only lie in its capacity to remove the cause of the interruption, so that the completeness of spontaneous life may be restored.

Action, then, is primary and thought is secondary. Thought

# THOUGHT AS SYMBOLIC INTERPRETATION

involves the cessation of action, and its function is to make possible the resumption of action. But now a curious problem confronts us. Thinking, though it results from the stoppage of activity, is itself an activity. What, then, is this activity which is not action? The answer is, I believe, that it is symbolic activity, or an activity of imagination. Since action is primary all our experience is necessarily active. With the stoppage of action at the primary level of immediate consciousness, the activity in which living consists is thrown back, as it were, upon itself. The stream of consciousness encounters an obstacle which dams its flow; and the waters, forced back upon themselves, pile themselves up against the obstacle until they can surmount it. This reflection, this turning back of life upon itself, involves the substitution of a new kind of activity which takes the place of what we usually call practical activity. The activity of thought is, therefore, a substitute activity which in reflection takes the place of and 'represents' the concrete activity of immediate life. Such an activity, since it performs no action in the concrete world, is properly described as unreal activity, not in the sense that it does not exist, but because it is deprived of the distinguishing property of concrete action—its capacity to determine changes in things. It has no causal efficacy in the real world. The changes which it effects are changes in images or ideas. And these images or ideas upon which the activity of thought is directed are substitutes for the real thing with which concrete action deals. It is by means of this substitution of images for things and through the manipulation of these images instead of the manipulation of things that thought performs its function of surmounting the obstacle to concrete action which has forced us into reflection. It is because thought is in this sense a substitute for action that its activity can be described as unreal or imaginary or symbolic or abstract.

At the root of this distinction between real and reflective activity lies the distinction between things and images. That distinction, however, is not so simple as is often supposed. When we are dealing with something concretely, it is there before our eyes. Under these conditions the image of the thing and the thing itself

# THOUGHT AS SYMBOLIC INTERPRETATION

are one and indistinguishable. But when we wish to consider anything which is not there, an image of the thing, which may or may not be identical with the percept of it, takes its place. We ought first, I think, to consider images which are identical with the things for which they are the substitutes, and to consider them in relation to their function in concrete life. Let me give you two examples. Fitzpatrick, in *Jock of the Bushveldt*, tells of his first lesson in hunting. On the long trek from the Cape into the interior it was the habit of the party, when camp was pitched, to go out singly in search of game for the pot. Like the others he went out with his rifle, time after time, and he alone came back uniformly empty-handed. One day, one of the old hunters took pity on him and suggested that they should go out together. For some time they walked without incident, till suddenly the older man seized him by the arm and whispered to him to stand absolutely still. Then he pointed to a clump of trees. 'There he is,' he whispered. Fitzpatrick searched the place with his eyes but could see nothing that even suggested an animal. The other proceeded to tell him exactly where to look and described to him the shape and colour that he was to look for. Then he suddenly saw, straight before him amongst the low trees, a large buck at which, in fact, he had been staring for some minutes without seeing it. After they had secured it, the older man remarked to Fitzpatrick: 'You'll never see them unless you have a picture in your mind of what they look like.' That is one of the primitive and most fundamental functions of the image. The image of anything guides perception in the search for the thing. It sets going a searching activity which, as it were, seeks something in the environment with which the image can coalesce and in which it can be absorbed.

Now take another example of a slightly different type. Suppose that you are standing opposite the point at which two roads meet, and you see two motor cars, one in either road, equally distant from the corner and travelling at the same speed. The drivers cannot see one another, and one of them is on the wrong side of the road. The image of the two cars and the cars themselves

## THOUGHT AS SYMBOLIC INTERPRETATION

which you see are identical. But in that situation imagination will probably shoot ahead of the fact and you will see the two cars collide at the corner before either of them has reached it. Suppose, then, that one of the cars suddenly stops before it reaches the corner. There is no collision. Yet you saw a collision. What, then, collided with what? I suppose the unsophisticated answer is that the two cars collided in your imagination, though of course they didn't really collide. As usual, the common-sense answer gets pretty near the truth. It is as though the image, which at first was indistinguishable from the percept, had suddenly slipped loose and developed itself as a continuation of what was happening, quicker than the movement of the actual objects before your eyes. In such a case consciousness develops the reality in image more quickly than the reality is itself developing, and so enables us to forecast the future, to anticipate in imagination what will happen later in reality. You will notice, too, in this example, how the possibility of error arises. Some of the essential factors, such as the intention of one of the drivers to stop his car, was absent from the image. And it was absent from the image because it was absent from the percept.

The next point to which I want to call attention is the *reduction of imagery*, or, as it is sometimes called, the process of abstraction. We have been considering cases in which the image is identical in appearance with the perceived thing. But this is not necessary. Much that is perceived, when we look at anything, is irrelevant to the recognition of it. An image, from which much of the perceptual detail has been omitted, will perform the normal functions of imagery. The omission of all irrelevant detail has one enormous advantage: it economizes effort. There is thus a tendency for the mind to reduce the images it employs to the bare minimum of detail which is necessary if they are to perform their function. And as more of the detail is left out, the image, while still functioning as a substitute for the thing, becomes more schematic and abstract. What is left out, and how much is left out, depends upon the particular purpose for which the image is required.

## THOUGHT AS SYMBOLIC INTERPRETATION

There are two results of this process of reduction to which we must attend. It leads, in the first place, to the generation of general, abstract images. The images of two different things may be reduced by the elimination of detail, for certain purposes, in such a way that they are identical. The result will be that the same image will serve equally well, again for certain purposes, as a substitute for several things. Such an image will serve equally well for the recognition of all things, in fact, whose images are capable of reduction to the same residue. It will serve as the mental substitute for any one of a class of things equally well, and so function as a generic image.

In the second place, the reduction of imagery may result in the production of symbols. In a very wide sense of the term, all images may be said to be symbols, since they are substitutes for the things of which they are images. But usually we employ the word in a narrower sense, to mean something that represents another thing without having an obvious resemblance to it. Such a symbol, if it is an image at all, cannot coalesce with the percept. It must, therefore, be recognized consciously as a representative of that which it symbolizes, if it is to fulfil its function. It is apt, therefore, to be considered as a mere conventional sign, arbitrarily chosen to represent the object. It may, indeed, in special cases, be purely conventional, as when we choose a name for a child. But such cases are rare and they cannot be primitive, since until we are familiar with the use of symbols which have created themselves, as it were, it could never occur to us to create them arbitrarily. It would seem that all reduced images must be in some sense parts of the apprehended characterization of the things of which they are images. But we must remember that in immediate experience things are not 'cut off with a hatchet' and that the concentration of attention which defines them against their background may take into focus more than we ultimately consider to be essential features of the object. The crown is part of the percept of the king when he wears it, and on ceremonial occasions it is the feature in the percept which distinguishes him from other men. The crown can, therefore, quite naturally

23

# THOUGHT AS SYMBOLIC INTERPRETATION

become the reduced image of the king. But when he puts off his crown the king is still the king. The crown is an occasional and accidental element in the percept of him, and when it is used to represent the king on occasions when he does not wear it, it has become, in a very simple fashion, a symbol.

The kind of symbolism with which we are directly concerned is the symbolism of language. Though the process by which it arises is more complicated, it is in principle the same. Words are reduced images which have become symbols. The sound which a child hears pronounced by an adult when he is looking intently at an object, is part of his total percept, and falls within the boundary, drawn by his attention, which includes the object as he sees it. The word, therefore, can, just like the crown, become the reduced image of the total percept, and so the symbol of the thing seen when it is employed as a substitute for it, even when the sound itself is not heard. Language is, therefore, a particular form, and the most generally useful form, of imagery which has been reduced in such a way that it forms a set of symbols.

The primary function of language is communication between persons. It is this purpose which governs its construction and its development. Any purpose for which language is used is, therefore, partially determined by this primary function. Any expression in words must be such that the language used is capable of being understood by someone else, even though the expression is not constructed for this purpose. That use of language, as a means of thought, which does not look beyond the expression of thought to its communication, is a secondary and derivative use of language, and is not necessarily so strictly bound by the necessities of communication. This is in some ways an advantage and in some ways a disadvantage to thought. Although in thinking we normally make use of the language symbolism, there are times when it is too coarse and too fixed to its common meaning to be entirely serviceable. It is apt to put a constraint upon thought and to hinder its creativeness. Language tends to stabilize and fossilize the analysis of the world which already been produced by thought and so to act as a conservative force. This

# THOUGHT AS SYMBOLIC INTERPRETATION

constraint is an advantage when it prevents vagueness in thinking and insists upon clear definition. It does this by insisting that thought should be expressed in such a way that it can be communicated. But this constraint also hampers the effort of discovery. A creative thinker seeking a new analysis of his data which is not yet common property and for which, therefore, the appropriate forms of language have not been discovered finds himself wrestling with language in an effort to constrain it to serve the purpose of expressing his thought. To do so he has continually to remodel language, to force words to bear a meaning to which they are not yet adapted or even to devise a new terminology of his own. It is not true that thought and its expression are the same thing. Expression is the result of thought. Though thought uses language as its instrument it is not completely at the mercy of the traditional meanings of words or of the traditional forms of analysis which are enshrined in the grammatical structure of language.

This fact makes it necessary to distinguish between words and ideas. The distinction is a difficult one to draw, mainly because over a wide field ideas and words have an inner identity. The case is similar to that of the relation between images and percepts. Words, in the first place, are public symbols, while ideas are private symbols. They both serve the same function as substitutes in imagination for something in reality to which they refer. In normal cases ideas are symbols which are meant to be communicated through language, so that an idea can be exchanged for a word whenever we desire to publish the idea, as it were. For this reason, we are accustomed to use the images of words as our ideas, or, at least, as the main constituents of our world of ideas. Within the limits of such normal thinking, we might define an idea as the image of a word, or rather, as the symbol of a word. For, in our thinking, any image which itself can be replaced by a word or its image will function in precisely the same way as the word itself, and simpler and subtler forms of imagery, such as kinæsthetic images, for example, are often much more perfect instruments of thought than the images of words can ever be. They are especially useful in those processes of thought which

## THOUGHT AS SYMBOLIC INTERPRETATION

there is no need to express publicly. We must remember that it is usually only the conclusion of a train of thought which is given public expression, and that even then it is only a fraction of what is present as idea in our mind that we utter in speech. Words and ideas, therefore, are generically the same. They are symbols which refer ultimately to the same world of concrete reality. The differences between them arise from the limitation imposed upon words by their primary function as means of communication.

It is important to notice that a symbol is only a symbol in terms of its function. A word, for example, is more than a sound. It can, of course, be treated as a sound but in that case it is no longer strictly a word. A word is a sound used. It is only when the sound is employed to stand for or represent something else that it is a symbol. A symbol is something used to represent something other than itself, and it is a symbol in virtue of this function, not at all because of its own characteristics as a thing. Indeed, a word need not be a sound in any sense. It may be written, and then it is a drawing. But the written word and the spoken word, although as things they are quite dissimilar, are yet the same word. This helps to explain why an idea may be an image of any kind, visual, auditory, kinæsthetic or any other, and still be the same idea. For, as we have seen, the idea is also a symbol and, therefore, it is an idea in terms of its use, that is to say, because it is referred to something other than itself. Completely different images may be the same idea just as a sound and a set of written characters may be the same word.

This discussion of the origin of abstract symbolic ideas and their relation to imagery in general enables us to understand the nature of reflective thought. We have seen how the energy that in its primary manifestation is the activity of life in action may be turned back upon itself, and so forced to find an outlet in an activity of the imagination. In such an activity the energy is real, but it is directed upon entities which are imaginary and symbolic. All activity must be directed upon something, and when it is debarred from exercising itself upon things, it must exercise itself upon imaginary things, upon substitutes for real things. We have

# THOUGHT AS SYMBOLIC INTERPRETATION

now seen what these substitute things are, and how they originate. They are images, either complete images or reduced images. We can say, therefore, that all reflective activity is activity directed upon images. It is the life-energy manipulating, in one way or another, those substitutes for real things which are the creatures of our imagination. Of these reflective activities thought is one of the most important. The term 'thought' is used in various senses. Sometimes it is used with a content so wide that it covers all the reflective activities including, for example, the activities of artistic imagination, or of mysticism. Normally, however, we restrict the term to those activities of reflection which are concerned with the solution of doubts and the achievement of intellectual knowledge through the processes of judgment and inference. In this sense, thought is a reflective activity directed upon ideas and manipulating ideas, and, therefore, it is closely associated with the symbolic images of language. It seeks its expression in words. It is to this aspect of reflective activity that our further study will be confined. But even so, there is a wider and narrower use of the term 'thought'. In its wider use it includes the processes by which ideas are substituted for things and expressed in words. These are the processes of description. In the narrower sense it excludes the processes of description and is confined to those activities of imagination which develop and organize the ideas which have been thus obtained. These are the processes of judgment and inference in their widest sense. We shall have to concern ourselves both with description and with judgment and inference, but only—this is a further limitation of our field—so far as they are deliberate and fully conscious.

The first element in the activity of reflective thought is the activity of description. By this I mean the activity through which an organized system of ideas, normally expressed in words, is substituted for the real world which we know in immediate experience and upon which our practical activity is directed. This activity involves first an analysis of the world we know. The unity of the world of perception has to be broken up, its elements isolated from one another and represented by separate symbols.

# THOUGHT AS SYMBOLIC INTERPRETATION

This analysis can be made in a large number of different ways. Indeed, if we looked no further, it could be carried out quite arbitrarily in an indefinite number of ways. But this arbitrariness is limited in practice by the purpose for which the analysis is made. And since that purpose has reference to real activity it is also limited by the nature of the real world. The process may be compared to the construction of a map. There, our purpose is to represent a tract of country on a reduced scale and in a schematic way. What is included in the map, or what is symbolized, is determined by the purpose for which the map is constructed. In any case, a vast mass of actual detail will be completely eliminated, so that what appears in the map is only a representation of so much of the actual country as is requisite for our purpose. Thus, the nature of the map is partly determined by us and partly by the nature of the country. The arbitrariness has its limits set by the use which is to be made of the map. Analytical description, which is the first of the activities of thought, is very like this. The main difference is that the symbols which we employ are ideas which have to be expressed in words and which for this reason are themselves usually images of words.

The main point we must notice is that descriptive analysis atomizes a reality which is given as a whole. The unity of the whole has, therefore, to be represented by arranging the isolated symbols in a relational system. This system of relations is not determined, at least directly, by the nature of the world as we experience it. It is itself a substitute, and in certain respects an inadequate substitute, for the given unity and completeness of immediate experience. The relational scheme which we use to make a systematic pattern of our symbols may vary according to the purpose for which it is used. In general, we may say that the main question for thought in the construction of its system is whether the system which it has constructed, both in regard to the degree of reduction to which the symbols have been submitted, and with regard to the pattern of their arrangement in the system, is or is not adequate. An idea or a system of ideas cannot in itself be either true or false. But it can be adequate or inade-

## THOUGHT AS SYMBOLIC INTERPRETATION

quate to the function which it was designed to fulfil. And if it is inadequate as a symbolic representation of the things which we wish to think about, it will almost certainly give rise to falsity in the processes of judgment which are based upon it.

This first activity of thought is concerned with substituting for the real world which we apprehend in immediate experience, a pattern of symbols which may serve as the representative or substitute for it in imagination, and which we can manipulate instead of the real world in our reflective activity.

The second group of activities which we have to consider, the activities of thought in the narrower sense, as judgment and inference, is concerned with the manipulation of the symbolic ideas which have been achieved through the process of analytic description. If we call the group of symbols which we manipulate in thinking the 'data', we may say that in thinking proper we are going beyond our data. Thought is always an advance in imagination beyond 'what is given'. It is important to remember that the given in any particular process of thought is not something absolute. It is that which is the starting point of thought relative to that particular activity of thinking. What is given for one process of thought may be itself the conclusion of some other process. Whatever is taken for granted or accepted as given in any judgment or inference is the given for that process. If we remember this we shall not fall into the trap of searching for an absolute given which can be regarded as the starting point of all thought. What is given in that sense is all that is known in immediate experience, and, as we have seen, it varies from individual to individual and from time to time with the growth of experience.

Now, since thinking is an activity of the imagination directed upon a given set of ideas, and since it consists in going beyond what is given to something that is in some sense new and not contained in what is given, it follows that the fundamental process of thought is the process of supposal. If I am in difficulty, for example, about how to achieve a certain end, I may suppose it achieved and then fill in, in imagination, the various steps which

## THOUGHT AS SYMBOLIC INTERPRETATION

will connect my present situation with the situation which I have imagined. This is a particularly obvious case. But for all that it is typical. So long as I am tied to the actual facts of the present situation in which I find myself, thinking is impossible. If I am in difficulty and so have an unresolved question before me, I cannot take practical action until the question is decided and the hesitation removed. The only action that I can take is imaginary action. The mere putting together of two premisses from which a conclusion can be drawn is itself an imaginative construction, for which no rules can be given. Once the premisses are taken together the conclusion follows, no doubt. But the uniting of the premisses is quite a different matter, and the capacity to see which data should be combined and how they should be combined is essential to all success in thinking. It is never discussed in textbooks of logic for the very good reason that it is dependent on the spontaneity of the mind, and no rules can be given for it.

The fundamental character of the imaginative act of supposal is concealed by the development of automatism in thought. The development of habits is essential in all rational action if only because it enables us to achieve an economy of action with regard to what is similar in different situations, and so to concentrate upon the differences which demand special consideration and a deliberate adaptation of action to the individual peculiarities of a new situation. The activities of thought are no exception. They depend equally upon the development of habit in the manipulation of ideas. So soon as an activity has become habitual, its performance is reduced to the level of mechanical repetition. Such automatic activity can obviously be formulated in a general law or rule of procedure. The laws of thought and their development as the principles of logic are simply the formulation of the rules which govern the activities of this particular use of the imagination so far as it depends upon habit. But no habitual action can lead to the discovery of what is not already known. It can only form the basis and the necessary basis for an activity which is not automatic but deliberate and consciously constructed. An activity of the imagination which has become habit-

## THOUGHT AS SYMBOLIC INTERPRETATION

ual ceases to be felt as an effort of the imagination just as an activity in concrete life which has become habitual ceases to involve any feeling of effort or strain. The consciousness of using our imagination is thus shifted to the particular points at which no rule can guide us, and we have to make a deliberate effort of construction. At these points we are aware that we are supposing, and the true characteristic of the process of thinking reveals itself.

It is possible to suppose almost anything. But it is not particularly useful to suppose things at random. If we are to use the capacity of imagining as a means for dealing with reality, it will have to be confined within the limits which make this possible. We shall have to suppose in such a way that conclusions can be drawn which it is possible to refer to reality. It will obviously be useless to suppose something that we know is not really possible. This provides the first limitation of the use of the imagination in thinking. We must limit it to the supposal of the possible. There is room here for a logical inquiry of considerable importance, which has not, so far as I know, been undertaken in any systematic way by logicians. It is the problem of the limits of legitimate hypothesis. It is possible to imagine situations for which there is no evidence, and draw conclusions. There is probably an element of this in all creative thinking. It is possible and also legitimate within limits to imagine, for purposes of thought, conditions which we know to be impossible, as when we imagine a particle of matter moving in space at an infinite distance from all other particles. It is not possible, on the other hand, to imagine the suspension of the law of gravitation and to draw any positive conclusion. The problem of the limits of legitimate supposal is not one that we need seek to solve here. But there is one point that is fairly obvious. A supposal which destroys any essential characteristic of reality as we know it, would destroy the basis for any conclusion about the nature of reality so far as we do not know it. And a supposal which contradicted the structure of the analytic description of something in reality, which is the starting point of an activity of thought, could not yield a conclusion which we should have any justification for referring to the reality about

## THOUGHT AS SYMBOLIC INTERPRETATION

which we are thinking. Even if, under such conditions, we could draw a conclusion at all, it would be a conclusion which contradicted its premisses. What is important here is to notice that what keeps the activity of the imagination within the limits of the necessary reference to reality is the retention throughout the process of thought of a structural basis which has itself been derived from reality by the process of analytic description. Within this fundamental structure we may suppose anything that seems useful, provided that the structure itself is not altered.

For this reason thought is controlled by a conception of unity. The main guarantee that the processes of imagination do not destroy the reference to reality which description has secured is that whatever changes the manipulation of ideas produces, they are not allowed to destroy the structural unity from which we started. The absence of contradiction, the maintenance of consistency, the securing of strict implication in the relation of consecutive stages in the thought-process are all aspects of this effort to maintain the unity of structure in a system of ideas from which we start, through the whole process of activity until the conclusion is reached. The preservation of this structural unity is not a complete guarantee, as we shall see. But without it there is little likelihood that the conclusion will be true. Within the thought-process itself it is the only guarantee. All other guarantees lie beyond the process of thinking itself.

This unity of structure, which is compatible with change in the ideas which it unifies, must obviously be a set of relations of an abstract and formal character. I propose to call it in subsequent chapters, which will consider different types of it, a unity-pattern. By this I mean that it is a formal conception of the way in which different symbols can be united so as to constitute a whole. We might call it a form of synthesis, as Kant did, or a schema of unity. But to call it a unity-pattern is simpler and carries fewer traditional implications. The unity of immediate experience, when it is broken by reflection and by the analysis of description, results in a set of symbolic images or ideas which are isolated from one another in the sense that it is in our power to arrange

# THOUGHT AS SYMBOLIC INTERPRETATION

them as we please. Before they can be used for the purpose for which they are designed, they must be arranged in a way that is determined by the reality which they are to represent. This, obviously, is only possible through some representation in imagination of the unity which is given in immediate experience itself. Essentially, as we have seen, that unity cannot be reproduced in reflection; it can only be represented by the synthesis of ideas in such a way that they form a whole. The unity-pattern is, thus, the conception of a unity constructed by the imagination. Without such a conception, which we can use as a rule to guide the imagination in the development of ideas, there could be no guarantee that the ideas were related in such a way that the result could be referred back to the concreteness of immediate experience. Without the unity-pattern, thought would be impossible. What we need to make thinking possible is, first, a pattern or a schema of relations, and, secondly, a set of symbolic images which can be arranged and rearranged within the pattern. To guide us in the manipulation of the symbols we have our knowledge of the purpose for which the activity is undertaken and of the need of so arranging the symbols that the pattern is, or can be, systematically completed.

There are certain fundamental patterns of this kind which represent the basic forms of the activity of thought. They define the line along which all other patterns must be developed and so determine in some sense the structure of the activity of thought itself. Their universality arises from the fact that they are dictated by the nature and function of thought in general, and by the nature of reality in general, which sets the problems with which thought has to deal. Such basic patterns are sometimes referred to as systems of categories. The laws of thought are determined by them, because such laws are the rules which the reflective activity of thinking must obey if it is to perform its function of overcoming the obstacles to practical activity in which thought originates and so succeed in setting us free to return from reflection to the activities of immediate experience which thought has interrupted. But before considering the three main unity-patterns

## THOUGHT AS SYMBOLIC INTERPRETATION

which determine the activities of thinking, we must complete our general discussion with an account of the process by which thought returns, when it is complete, to the reality of immediate experience from which it arose. This return of thought to reality is usually described as the process of verification.

THREE

# Interpretation and Verification

Having considered how thought arises out of immediate experience, and the process in which it consists, we must consider next the return of thought to immediate experience when the activity of reflection has reached its conclusion. It will be well to summarize in a few words the main argument, so far as it has gone, so that we may make the connexion clearly.

We have seen that thought is not the only way to knowledge, since there must be knowledge before there can be thought. Thought is always about something that is known. We have seen also that thought arises from a failure in the process of concrete life-activity, which brings it to a stop and transfers its energy from the field of concrete reality to the field of imagery. Thought is, therefore, one form of the manipulation of images. What distinguishes it from other forms is the purpose which governs it and the function which it fulfils in personal life. The rationality of thought, therefore, depends upon its capacity to achieve its purpose and to fulfil its function. As that function is to overcome an obstacle to concrete activity, the rationality of thought is bound up with the reference of its images and systems of images to the reality that they symbolize, a reference which is not theoretical but practical.

Now, in the actual process of thinking, once the symbol-system of description has been set up, we immerse ourselves in a world of

## INTERPRETATION AND VERIFICATION

imagery. The manipulation of images is carried on in terms of the rules of the thought-process, which are partly inherent in the imagination and partly habits which have been developed by experience and training. The conclusions we reach are the results of this development of symbols. It is obviously important to discover how far we can trust these processes of the imagination to produce as their final result an expression which is appropriately related to the reality to which we wish to refer it. We shall have to ask, in other words, how the truth of a conclusion can be guaranteed.

The problem of truth, it has often been pointed out, is really the problem of error. We must begin by discovering how it is that error may arise in the process of thinking. Now, to be in error, we have to believe that a statement is true when it is not. We cannot be in error and know that we are in error. A statement is a symbolic expression. To think that it is true is to accept it as appropriately symbolizing something that belongs to the world of immediate experience. If it is false it does not properly symbolize that to which we refer it. The question is, then, how there can arise in the process of thought symbolic expressions which cannot be properly referred to reality. When we have seen how this is possible, we shall be in a position to ask in what this reference to reality consists and how its appropriateness can be tested.

One fact that has been brought out by our earlier discussions is that thinking is a particular form of the use of imagination; a specialization, for a particular purpose, of our power to form and combine images. We know, too, that the imagination has the capacity to combine elementary images, all of which are derived in the last resort from the characters which the world presents to our perception, into a composite image quite unlike anything we know in concrete experience. If thought is a particular use of this capacity, we need not be surprised that error arises, that the thought-processes may result in a combination of symbols which is not found in real experience and which, therefore, cannot be referred to anything real. The marvel is rather that we can ever manipulate images, combining and recombining them in novel

# INTERPRETATION AND VERIFICATION

ways, and find that the pattern we have constructed does result, in spite of the play of imagination which has produced it, in a complex symbol which can sometimes be directly referred to reality. The wonder is that our judgments are ever true.

We need not attempt to analyse exhaustively the different ways in which error can arise. We might note that there may be errors of description. The actual process of substituting a symbolic pattern for the concrete reality which it represents may be badly performed. There may also be error in the thinking process. We may fail to manipulate the symbol-pattern according to the rules for its manipulation. Consider the solution of a simple problem by algebra. (The fact that the problems which we solve in this way are usually already symbolized in language and retranslated into mathematical symbols makes no difference in principle, and simplifies the example.) The first task is to construct the equations which represent the concrete situation or as much of it as is considered relevant. This is often a matter of some difficulty. It involves the selection of, what is relevant in the problem as well as its analysis in terms of unit-entities. We may fail to construct the proper equation and be unaware that we have failed. In that case, we will get error in the conclusion, however correct our manipulation of the symbols may be in terms of the rules of algebra. We may also get the equations right and make a mistake in working them out. That also will vitiate the conclusion. These two stages are really different. When the equations are being constructed the mind goes back and forward between the concrete problem and the symbolism. Our concern is to see that the reference from symbol to reality is correct, that the symbolic expressions which we write down really do symbolize the concrete situations which we want them to represent. But when we have got our equations we dismiss the concrete situation from our minds. We turn to the manipulation of symbols, and what now guides our activity is no longer the concrete facts but the rules of algebra. It is only when this working is complete that we turn once more to the concrete problem and reinterpret our symbolic conclusions in terms of it. We may note, however, several

37

## INTERPRETATION AND VERIFICATION

interesting points about this example before passing on. The first is that these two stages—the descriptive and the manipulative—need not be absolutely separate. They may interpenetrate. It is not necessary that the process of description should be completed before the manipulation of the symbols begins. In fact, it is only in the simplest cases that this is possible. Usually we must carry in our mind, even if it is only vaguely, the meaning of the symbols, that is to say, the concrete situation to which they refer, to guide the process of manipulation. If we do not, two kinds of difficulty are liable to arise. One is that at points in the manipulation, where there is a choice between different ways of procedure, we may have nothing to guide our choice, and so may follow a line of working which leads nowhere, or rather, which leads to a conclusion which is of no use to us, however correct it may be. The second is that the rules themselves may let us down. Mathematical thought has its limitations. It is only adequate, as we shall see later, for dealing with the finite. Against the intrusion of the infinite into our symbols we can only be protected by remembering what they stand for. The simple method of proving, according to the rules of algebra, that one is equal to two is a good example of this.[1] It is possible because where $x$ is equal to $a$ we introduce the factor $x - a$ into the equation. Unless we remember that $x$ and $a$ stand for the same thing numerically, we do not notice that $x - a = 0$ and, unawares, we introduce an infinite factor into the equation to which the ordinary rules do not apply.

Another interesting point is this. We often find that there are several solutions of our equations, all of which are equally correct, but some of which have no conceivable reference to the concrete problem with which we started. We get results, for example, which involve a meaningless symbol like $\sqrt{-1}$. The rules of manipulation applied to a symbolic expression constructed purely to represent a concrete situation have the power

---

1. Let $x = a$. Then $x^2 = ax$, $x^2 - ax = ax - a^2$
   $(x - a)(x + a) = a(x - a)$
   $x + a = a$, $2a = a$, $2 = 1$.

## INTERPRETATION AND VERIFICATION

to generate symbolic expressions which have no reference to reality at all. We need not examine this curious fact further than to note that the capacity to generate such unreal entities is characteristic of the imagination. Our trouble in thinking rationally is to eliminate as far as possible this 'artistic' element, or, as we might call it, this 'creative' element, from those processes of the imagination which we call thinking. Here, again, what is curious is not that such irrational conclusions can arise, but that we can so far harness the spontaneity of imagination that they arise so infrequently and in such a way that they can be detected and eliminated.

Another difficulty, however, and one which gives rise to positive error, arises when the symbolism we use is inadequate to the purpose for which we use it. We shall consider some major examples of this later, when we discuss the efforts that have been made to use the symbolism of mathematical and biological thought for the philosophical purpose of interpreting the universe. These forms of symbolism are adequate to deal with limited fields of experience, but when they are applied to the universe as a whole the infinite factor inevitably enters and the rules of manipulation no longer give correct results. But there is one universal aspect of this difficulty which affects all thinking. All thought involves generalization, and it is never safe, as the proverb says, to generalize. The reason for this is a simple one. A symbol always involves the reduction of the content of an image, and the possibility of using the same symbol to refer to a number of different things depends upon the possibility of reducing their content in imagination to a point at which what remains is the same in all cases. We saw also that it is only for certain purposes that this is possible. As a result, the use of general ideas is always liable to give rise to error. A general symbol may be used in cases where the differences between the particulars that it groups together as identical are not irrelevant. This danger is enhanced by the process of generalization in thinking. The description of any class of things must inevitably be achieved by reference to only a small number of the members of the class. This symbolic

## INTERPRETATION AND VERIFICATION

description is generalized when it is taken for granted that it will apply to *all* members of the class, many of which are unknown, and may, indeed, be future members of the class which, as yet, are non-existent. Our immediate experience provides us with a general justification of generalization because it reveals the infinite in the finite. It is this that is represented in reflection by the relation of the universal and the particular. But it cannot justify any particular generalization since that always depends, partly at least, on our own selection of what we think is relevant to our purpose. We are, therefore, always liable to over-generalize, that is to say, to apply a description or a conclusion which we know to be true in certain cases to all cases which we take to be included in the same class. It is customary to formulate this by saying that what is true in certain particular cases will be true for all similar cases. In this way it is always possible to produce a verbal defence of generalization. You have only to say, if the conclusion turns out to be inapplicable to a new case, that the new case is not really similar. But that is merely playing with words. For purposes of classification two things are similar only from a particular point of view, or for a particular purpose. When we over-generalize, we do so in terms of a purpose. Our symbolic statement will express within the limits of its purpose all the things which immediate experience reveals as similar. We know that these similars are different in other respects. We believe that their differences are, for our purpose, irrelevant. Sometimes it turns out that this is not really the case.

Against this danger of over-generalization thought itself can provide no guarantee. The description may be thoroughly adequate to the case by reference to which it is constructed. The manipulation of the symbols may be entirely correct according to the rule of the unity-pattern which it employs. The conclusion, however, since it is generalized, that is to say, since it is referred to new cases which are assumed to be similar but which have not been examined, may turn out to be invalid. For this reason the truth of no conclusion whatsoever can be completely guaranteed. We can never be sure that it will be possible to refer it to reality in

## INTERPRETATION AND VERIFICATION

the way in which it demands to be referred. The only way to secure certainty in a conclusion is to abstain from referring it to reality. But a conclusion which is not referred to reality is neither true nor false. It is merely a symbol lying unused. At most we may say that it is correct. It is this fact more than any other that forces upon us the necessity for verifying all conclusions. There is no way whatsoever of guaranteeing the truth of any conclusion in terms merely of the reflective processes by which it has been reached. The conclusion, we say, refers to reality. It would be more proper to say that it demands to be referred. The nature of reflective knowledge is such that it is always incomplete until we have returned from the reflective process to the concreteness of immediate experience. Our study has shown us that this means returning from thought to action.

The necessity for the verification of all conclusions is now completely recognized in the scientific field. In other fields it is still unrecognized or even denied. It will be well then, to consider the place that verification holds in science first of all, in order to bring out the implications of its acceptance. Verification is primarily a return from thought to action, in order to find in the immediate experience of concrete activity a justification for accepting the conclusions which have been reached through the manipulation of ideas in the thought-processes. The implications of this are far-reaching. In the first place it implies a distrust of speculative thought. To accept the necessity of verification means more than to recognize the possibility of mistakes in thinking. These, after all, could be discovered and avoided by better thinking. It involves rather the belief that thought alone, however correct it may be, cannot guarantee its own conclusions. It means that all conclusions must be regarded as hypothetical.

The second implication is that in order to guarantee conclusions, there must be a return from the abstract to the concrete and that the only way in which this is possible is through practical activity. I emphasize this point because verification is always misrepresented as a reference from thought to sense-perception. It is not merely this, and not essentially this. It is a return to the

## INTERPRETATION AND VERIFICATION

field of immediate experience in which consciousness is only the cognitive aspect of practical activity. When we treat a conclusion as hypothetical, and so demand that it should be verified, we imply something like this: 'If my conclusion is true, then if I act upon it I shall have a certain experience which I can forecast.' In other words, 'if I do something I shall get a certain result'. In experiment I test the result of a process of thought by its capacity to perform its fundamental function of making successful action possible. If, then, I perform the action which the conclusion suggests, and discover that in my concrete activity I do not get the result that the conclusion warranted me in expecting, then I know that there is error involved in the conclusion. That is the essence of experimental verification. This accords with the analysis of reflection in the last chapter. Thought arises from failure in concrete practical life. The failure sets going a process of symbolic activity in the imagination. The function of this process is to overcome the obstacle and so to enable us to resume action successfully. It follows that the test of the success of our thinking lies precisely in our capacity to do something as a result of our thinking that we were unable to do before. Experiment is, therefore, the only way in which we can discover whether our thinking has fulfilled its function, and so test the truth of its conclusion.

But there is a third implication. The failure of an experiment disproves the truth of the theory on which it was based, but the success of an experiment does not prove the truth of anything. There is a simple reason for this. The conclusion is general. The experiment is a particular action. It may quite well be that another action based upon the same theory would have failed. To accept an experiment as a conclusive proof of the truth of a theory would involve a generalization which itself requires testing. It would imply the assumption that I shall always be successful in acting upon this conclusion because I have been successful in acting upon it in this particular case. Such a conclusion cannot be guaranteed. The risk of over-generalization cannot be avoided.

Now, this may seem a completely sceptical conclusion. It means that no experiment can ever guarantee the truth of a

# INTERPRETATION AND VERIFICATION

conclusion. If thought cannot guarantee truth and experiment cannot either, what guarantee of truth can there be? The question implies the very theory of knowledge which we have discarded. It implies that the function of thought is to provide us with knowledge which is fixed, absolute and finally guaranteed. Such knowledge, we have seen, so far as it is possible or desirable, belongs to our immediate experience and is not the result of reflection. This enables me to state the fourth and most important implication of the scientific use of experimental verification. Knowledge, in so far as it is the result of processes of reflection, does not involve certainty. In this field, certainty is precisely what we cannot have and what we should not look for. What the verification of thought does provide, and what we have a right to expect from it, is a continuous development in the rationality of our beliefs, which in its turn makes possible a continuous development in the rationality of concrete human activity. The positive thing that the process of verification does is to link together thought and action. By doing this it provides an increasing basis of support in the concrete field of practical experience for theoretical conclusions. A rational belief is not a belief which is known to be certainly true. It is simply a conclusion which it is reasonable to believe. And it is reasonable to believe a conclusion when the evidence in its favour is greater than the evidence in favour of any other suggested alternative. It is this that verification through action achieves.

Science has secured a continuity in the development of theory. The same fundamental hypothesis forms the basis of thought and experiment for all scientists, and by their thought and experiments material is gathered for its modification. As a result there arises an interlocking body of theory, each part of which supports the other parts, so that all evidence which tells in favour of one element in the theoretical structure is a reason, so far as it goes, for accepting the whole. A situation must soon arise in which it is almost always far more reasonable to believe the official theory than any isolated and speculative hypothesis which is independent of the accumulated body of evidence, simply because the evidence in favour of the official theory is so overwhelming. This

## INTERPRETATION AND VERIFICATION

does not mean that the official theory is necessarily true and the isolated hypothesis necessarily false. The contrary sometimes turns out to be the case. It means only that it will be more rational to believe the official theory, even if it happens to be false; because it is supported by a far more complete analysis of the facts, and a much richer and more varied range of experimental verification. This applies, of course, only to such knowledge as is the result of thinking. It does not apply to what is known in immediate experience. When theory, even official theory, flies in the face of immediate experience, it is simply false, and that is the end of the matter. There can be no arguing with facts; though scientists, like other people, may sometimes be tempted to turn a blind eye to them.

The conclusion we have to draw, however, is that verification is an essential part of any process of reflection which can claim to be deliberate and rational. At present, we are prepared to accept this conclusion within the limited sphere of scientific investigation. Beyond that field we are apt to deny both its possibility and its necessity. I am concerned to insist that there can be no such limitation; that no process of thinking has any claim upon our belief unless it is supported by, and appeals to, verification in action.

I should like to call your attention here to the fact that in science itself there is a limitation of the process. Science tends to reverse the true relation between thought and action, by making action subordinate to thought. We do this whenever we make knowledge an end in itself. The scientist uses experiment as a means to the extension of reflective activity. If he insists on practical verification, and so turns from thought to action, it is in order to return again from the field of practical activity to the more comfortable field of reflection. He uses action—a very limited form of action—as a means to reflection. But the real verification of scientific theory is to be found only when science itself is used as a means to the development of concrete life. It is in the application of science to the development of civilization and to the extension of human control over the forces of nature, that the real verification of scientific conclusions is to be found. The common sense of mankind recognizes this. The belief in

## INTERPRETATION AND VERIFICATION

science which has become so widespread in our time is based, and rightly based, upon the application of science to concrete human purposes. It is in this field, not in the laboratory, that science has to prove its theories, and also to discover its limitations. But how, you might ask, can there be experiment and verification of our reflective conclusions outside the field of science? How, for instance, is a philosophical theory to be verified? I shall answer in the first place that philosophy is always verified, even if unconsciously, in the process of individual and social history. It is, of course, possible to speculate philosophically for the sake of speculating, and to prevent our conclusions from affecting practical activity. Such philosophy is not serious. It is a kind of game which certain people play. We are not concerned with sport, but with the serious business of thought. When philosophy is taken seriously it is bound to affect our immediate experience of living and to verify itself in the satisfactoriness of the life-experience which it helps to produce. In the social field, too, philosophy undergoes a constant process of verification. The way in which a society organizes and conducts its social life is always the unconscious expression of a philosophical conception of the world. The breakdown of European life in the eighteenth century, as illustrated, for example, by the fury of the French Revolution, by the scepticism of Hume and Voltaire, or by the cynicism of *Gulliver's Travels*, is itself the discovery of the practical failure of the philosophy by which Europe had lived since the Reformation. And the collapse in our own time is another instance of an unsuccessful experiment in philosophy. But such experiments are not deliberate. They produce no satisfactory judgment upon philosophical theory, because the theories themselves which they unconsciously test are not explicitly recognized. It is only when an experiment is deliberately undertaken on a basis of theory for the purpose of discovering what that theory will enable us to do that we could not do before, or not so successfully, that it fulfils the function of verification in the life of deliberate reflection. How is that possible? Of the many possible answers I shall give only one. There is at present going on in Russia a vast experiment in the deliberate

## INTERPRETATION AND VERIFICATION

creation of a new type of social life. That experiment is consciously and explicitly based upon a philosophical theory, and the phases of its development are deliberately guided by the philosophical theory upon which it is based. We have here, therefore, the first attempt that man has made on a large scale in the deliberate verification of a philosophical conclusion. The thing is possible because it is being done. If it is possible to verify the Hegelian dialectic in this way, it must be possible to verify other philosophical conclusions in a similar way. Whether we are prepared to do it or not is another matter. But, in any case, I think we may conclude that until something of this kind becomes possible and is carried out, we cannot expect the beginnings of a developing body of philosophical theory which is more than speculative and, therefore, more than guesswork or phantasy. We should remember in this connexion that, by abstaining from deliberate experiment in the philosophical field, we do not escape from the unconscious verification of our various philosophies; we merely relinquish the effort to control their verification in a rational fashion. It would seem as if history were driving us, under pressure of necessity, to attempt the deliberate planning of our social life. The theoretical basis of such an effort at social reconstruction must be philosophical. If the philosophy which guides it is unconscious, we shall be at the mercy of unconscious forces, which, because they are unconscious, are uncontrollable.

FOUR

# Mathematical Thought and Mechanism

So far our discussion has been general. I have argued that thought is not a self-contained activity of knowing but a symbolic activity of the imagination. Its rationality depends upon its relation to the immediate experience of living and the knowledge which arises in, and is an inseparable part of, that experience. It is rational only in relation to its function, only in so far as its symbolic activity is objective. And that objectivity depends upon the way in which its symbols and symbol-patterns refer to the real world of concrete experience.

The main difference which we discovered between the symbol-world and the real world to which it refers lies in the nature of the unity which each possesses. The unity of immediate experience is a given unity, given in the apprehension of the infinite in the finite. But the unity of the world of symbols is a constructed unity, a synthesis of elements which have been obtained through an analysis of the given. Now, the construction of a synthesis of elements depends upon the representation of unity. It implies the presence of an idea of structure through which isolated symbols can be bound together to form a whole. The representation of this idea of a whole is what I have called a schema or pattern of unity. Its function is to guide the activities of the imagination, in its efforts to combine symbols or ideas, in such a way that their combination shall produce such a map of reality or of some part or aspect of reality as will serve the purposes for which thought is undertaken.

## MATHEMATICAL THOUGHT AND MECHANISM

In this chapter I wish to consider the most general and, therefore, the most abstract of the unity-patterns which thought employs. I refer to the mechanical unity-pattern of mathematical thought. Like all the principles of symbolic construction, this one is determined by the purpose which underlies it, and by the function which it serves in personal life. It arises from the necessity of manipulating physical objects and is, therefore, adapted to the representation of reality so far as reality is stuff to be used, or to put it more technically, so far as reality is material. The idea of matter is the idea of stuff, of raw material which is formed in accordance with our purposes by our action upon it. When, therefore, we represent the world as matter, we are representing it as the field in which we exercise constructive activity, as that which we use for productive purposes.

When we are interested in anything as material to be used, we are not interested in it for its own sake. The value which it has for us is an economic value, that is to say a utility-value, a value which is derived entirely from the purpose for which the thing is to be used. But to use things we must understand them, within limits. We must understand what they can be used for, and this understanding depends upon a knowledge of those characteristics which make them usable for one purpose or another. Any characteristics which they possess that have no use-value we shall ignore. Now, the characteristics of anything which make it utilizable are its causal properties, and, therefore, the understanding of things from the point of view of their economic value will be limited to an understanding of their causal properties.

Suppose, then, that the reflection which lies at the basis of an activity of thought is caused by a failure in our use of things in an immediate practical activity. The thought that results will be concerned to represent and to interpret reality as matter, and so to understand reality as a set of causal properties which can, if properly understood, be utilized for practical purposes. There are two main points to notice here. The first is that in such thinking any individual thing will be symbolized not for its individuality but merely as a bearer of general properties. For when we wish to

## MATHEMATICAL THOUGHT AND MECHANISM

use anything we are concerned merely with the general characteristics which enable us to use it. If there are other objects possessing the same characteristics, they are all equally useful as instruments for our purpose, and any one of them will serve just as well as any other. It follows that in such a case the same symbol can be used to represent all objects which have the same general characteristics and, therefore, the same causal properties.

In the second place, things which are considered from the material point of view are considered in terms of what they can do. They are means to certain ends. When we cease acting and withdraw ourselves from the use of things, the conception of means and ends, which is a practical conception, gives place to the conception of cause and effect, because we have ceased to be agents. In reflection upon the world as matter, therefore, whatever we consider will appear as the cause of an effect or as the effect of a cause, and whether it appears as cause or as effect will be purely a question of the order in which it is taken relatively to other things. Everything from this point of view is either cause or effect as you please to take it. Further, since we are not really concerned with anything as this individual thing, but merely as a bearer of general properties, the understanding of its causality will be an understanding of its general causal properties. This means that what we are concerned to represent and understand are the general principles of causal relation. I say 'relation', because the idea of using a thing commits us to considering it essentially in relation to something else, never in and for itself.

We have here, then, a type of reflection which is at once limited in its scope and yet of universal application. It is limited because it considers everything from a limited point of view. It is universal because everything in the world can be considered from this limited point of view. Everything, that is to say, is at least material, however much more it may be. Everything can be considered as potentially usable. What we have now to discover is the unity-pattern which is demanded as the basis of symbolic construction in this type of reflection.

The unity-pattern must be completely general for the whole

## MATHEMATICAL THOUGHT AND MECHANISM

type of thought to which it belongs. It has to represent, for that type of thought, the way in which any symbol-element whatever can be built together in imagination so as to form a unitary whole. It cannot take account of the particular nature of the elements which it brings together, since these vary from occasion to occasion and the pattern must be the same for all occasions. It follows that the unity-pattern will abstract completely from all but the absolutely universal characteristics of the things which are organized as symbols within it. Now we have seen that when we consider things as material, we are concerned with them merely as bearers of causal properties. Different things will, of course, be bearers of different causal properties since they cannot all be used in the same way. In practice we shall find ourselves dealing with classes of things, and each member of any class will have the same causal properties as every other member of the same class. To reach the complete abstraction of the unity-pattern we shall have to disregard such differences between different classes of things and consider only what everything has in common, so far as it is material. This will be simply the fact that it is a bearer of causal properties. We have made a complete abstraction of all the particular causal properties of different things; so that every particular thing, merely because it is material, is of the same type as every other, and, therefore, everything can be represented, at the limit of material abstraction, by the same symbol. This symbol is the unit. Every thing is one thing.

From this completely abstract point of view reality as material appears as an infinite assemblage of units, and, therefore, any finite part of it, as a definite number of units. It follows from this that anything, so far as it is material, can be represented as an assemblage of identical units and that the rule of construction for its symbolic representation is given in the formula 'one plus one equals two'. This rule means that any material whole can be represented symbolically as a unity produced by the repetition of identities. Pure mathematics, which explores the possible patterns which can be constructed on the basis of this rule, is the technique for the manipulation of this symbolism.

# MATHEMATICAL THOUGHT AND MECHANISM

We see, then, that mathematical thought is concerned with the expression in symbolic form of the nature of reality in so far as it is material. In itself, pure mathematics can be neither true nor false. It may, of course, be correct or incorrect, since in its elaboration we may inadvertently be false to the basic rule of construction which underlies it. Nothing can be true or false except in terms of its reference as a pattern of symbols to something which it symbolizes. Until the completely abstract formulæ of pure mathematics are referred to concrete reality and so used for the interpretation of the world, the question of their truth cannot arise.

The postulate which underlies the use of mathematical thought, and which expresses the condition under which its unity-pattern can be applied, is this: 'Any whole given in experience can be represented in imagination as a complex of unit-elements and these elements can be represented as bare identities or units. The complex as a whole can then be represented as the sum of these units.' This postulate determines the method of analysis which is employed in describing the reality under consideration. It must be analysed atomically, and the atoms composing it must be represented as identical. Elements in the given which cannot be so analysed must either be disregarded or correlated with elements which can be so analysed. How far reality will submit to this analysis without vitiating the symbolic activity which is based upon it, is a matter which can only be discovered empirically. As a result, the processes of thought which are based upon the symbolism can never produce conclusions which are more than probable. The possibility that elements in the given which have been ignored or misrepresented may be essential to the correctness of the result is always present. Therefore, such results have always to be tested by practical experiment before they can be considered even provisionally valid.

This representation of complex objects as constituted by the repetition of identities has certain difficulties inherent in it. In the first place, the idea of a repetition of identical elements is itself irrational. If they are really identical they are one and not two. If

## MATHEMATICAL THOUGHT AND MECHANISM

they are really two they are different things. How can two things be identically the same and yet different? Yet this is how mathematical symbolism must represent things. The answer which suffices for the purposes of mathematical thought is that two elements identical in nature may differ merely by their position in space or in time. They may be arranged side by side in space, or repeated in succession in time. It is important to notice that this implies that space and time are themselves nonentities, that they make no difference of any kind to the identities which are arranged in them; and 'that which makes no difference' is as good a definition as we could wish of the unreal. This answer, therefore, is not theoretically satisfactory. It involves a contradiction in terms. But it is *practically* satisfactory for the purpose of this type of thought, for a reason which we have already discovered. To treat anything as material is to treat it in terms of what it can be used for. And in terms of its use one thing can be identical with another because it can be used for the same purpose. For purposes of buying and selling one sixpence is identical with any other. The question of individual differences between the coins is irrelevant. We may, therefore, pass this particular difficulty by. But it reveals the fact that in the nature of things a mathematical interpretation of reality must be a limited interpretation. It can only be valid from a particular point of view and for particular purposes.

When thinking mathematically, then, we have to represent objects as complexes of identical elements so that they may be manipulated in idea in accordance with the rule that one plus one equals two. The use of such a pattern of symbolism raises certain problems of first-rate importance. We find ourselves working with the idea of a number of elements, all treated as identical, arranged in some order in space. There is nothing in the symbols to represent the qualitative differences in the object symbolized. The object itself is immediately known as a complex of different qualities. Some of these, because they are causal properties or at least the signs of causal properties, such as weight or temperature, are essential to our problem. They must, therefore, be represented or symbolized in some way, and there is only one way

# MATHEMATICAL THOUGHT AND MECHANISM

in which this can be done. They must be represented by the *order* in which the unit-elements are arranged relatively to one another. All qualitative differences in the object, which cannot be considered irrelevant, must be symbolized in this fashion. The differences between objects must be represented as differences either in the number of unit-elements in each or in the order in which the unit-elements are arranged in each. There is, by hypothesis, no difference between the units themselves. They are always the same and always identical with one another. But there may be more of them in the complex, or they may occupy different relative positions within the space which is occupied by the complex.

We must now remind ourselves that the purpose of this symbolism is to enable us to understand the causality of things or the ways in which they act upon one another. Causality is obviously bound up with change, and, therefore, the representation of change is fundamental to mathematical thought. How, then, is change to be represented? For change implies a difference in the same thing at different times. Obviously, since there can be no difference in the elements into which we have analysed the objects we are considering, any change in these must be represented as a change in the relative positions of the elements which compose them. It will be a difference in the arrangement of the same elements. All change must be represented in this type of symbolism in this particular way, because there is no other way in which it can be represented.

It is at this point that the *problem* of causality emerges. To understand change, we must be able to account for its occurrence. Now, in the practical experience which gives rise to mathematical thought the explanation of change is simple. We use material things for our purposes. Matter, as that which is used, is passive to the activity we exercise upon it. But in reflection we have stopped acting and are considering changes that *occur* to material objects apart from our activities upon them. From the reflective point of view, changes *happen* to things, and we are driven to account for their happening. But we have represented things as arrangements of identical elements in space. In this

53

# MATHEMATICAL THOUGHT AND MECHANISM

representation there is absolutely nothing to account for any change. There is nothing to account even for the arrangement itself, apart from any change in it. The arrangement will not explain itself, the space in which the elements are arranged, being characterless, will not explain the arrangement, nor will the elements themselves, since they are bare units and identical. It follows that the source of any change in the arrangement must be looked for outside the complex; in other words, that the cause of the change must be external to the thing that is changed. The symbolism of mathematical thought forces us to represent all change as determined by an external cause and, therefore, all action as mechanical action. This leads us to notice what is essential to the conception of mechanism. Mechanical action is action in which all change is the effect of a cause external to that which is changed and in which, therefore, the changes of an object and so all its activities are determined not by its own nature but by a force acting upon it from outside. The object is conceived as essentially passive. It is, therefore, incapable of originating its own changes. So that all that it does must be referred to something other than itself which acts upon it. Another way of stating this is to say that mathematical thought, because of the nature of its symbolism, must represent all change (and, therefore, all action) as completely determined. Determinism and mechanism are, in fact, the same thing. They both mean that an observed change is to be referred not to the nature of that which changes but to something other than itself which acts upon it.

This enables us to state the inherent limitation of mathematical thought in another way. Since whatever is represented through mathematical symbolism must have its activities referred beyond itself, it necessarily presupposes the existence of something which is not and cannot be represented in the symbolism. Any attempt to use mathematical thought as a final explanation of the nature of reality must inevitably be involved in an infinite regress. However far you cast your net, however much you include in your system of symbols, it will remain true that your representation refers you beyond itself to an external cause. A mechanical

# MATHEMATICAL THOUGHT AND MECHANISM

and deterministic interpretation of the universe, such as mathematical analysis imposes upon the mind, must, if it is taken as a final and complete explanation, be self-contradictory. For in claiming completeness it claims to include everything within it, while its form compels it to refer whatever it includes to something beyond it. It is involved both in asserting and in denying the existence of something beyond. If there is something beyond what it represents it is no longer complete; if there is nothing beyond it, what is represented must, as a whole, be self-determining in its activity and, therefore, not mechanical.

We can now answer the final question: 'What kind of interpretation of the universe will be provided by mathematical thought, and how far will it be adequate to the world as we know it?' We have to notice that all thought is mathematical in type if it uses as its basis of analysis the unity-pattern which we have described. It need not necessarily employ pure mathematics as its instrument, though it will be most accurate and reliable when it does. What is fundamental to mathematical thought is the analysis of the object into a set of unit-elements and their arrangement in an order. Such an analysis forces upon us, through the nature of the abstractions employed, a mechanical interpretation of action. It follows that any interpretation of the universe which is based upon this type of symbolic representation must represent the universe as a mechanism in which all action is completely determined in accordance with causal laws. If such an interpretation is offered as a philosophy we have what is called 'materialism'. We may, therefore, assert that all philosophy which is based on thought of the mathematical type, if it is consistent, must be materialistic. This would include the whole of modern philosophy prior to Kant, even the philosophies of Berkeley or Spinoza. We might add that any philosophy which bases itself upon science must necessarily be of this type. For all science, so far as it is really science, rests upon the schematism of mathematical thought.

The analysis of mathematical thought enables us to conclude that materialism must be false because it is inherently self-contradictory. It implies the universality of mechanistic determinism

# MATHEMATICAL THOUGHT AND MECHANISM

as an explanation of action. To account for an action mechanically is to account for it in terms of a force acting upon it from outside. To interpret the universe in mechanistic terms, therefore, is to interpret it in terms of something beyond it which acts upon it. But by definition there can be nothing outside the universe to act upon it. Mathematical thought can only be applied to finite systems falling within a wider environment. Its presupposition is that there must be a source of energy outside the system which it analyses and seeks to understand. It cannot, therefore, be applicable to the universe as a whole. In other words, philosophical thought cannot be valid if it is mathematical in type.

We can see this more correctly if we return to the point from which we started. Mathematical thought, and therefore science, arises from a particular kind of concrete situation. It arises from our interest in using things, and applies only to things in so far as they are utilizable. That is why it issues in materialism. The conception of matter is the general conception of things as material or stuff. Clay, for example, is the material or stuff which the potter uses to make his pots. And it is called matter or stuff precisely because it is passive to the action which he exercises upon it. The universe as matter is the universe as stuff which is passive to action, and the very conception implies an agent or source of action outside it and acting upon it. Matter is essentially a relative conception. It is relative to an agent that uses it. There can, in the strict sense, be no such thing as a material cause, though there may be a material instrument. For 'matter' means that in which effects are produced, and 'cause' means that which produces effects. By definition, therefore, the conception of cause is inapplicable to matter. That which is cause is necessarily the agent, while matter is that which is the patient. The agent is that which acts; matter is that which is acted upon. Therefore, the conception of a universe which is material and nothing more can only arise through a misunderstanding. It would have to be a universe in which there was nothing to act, and in which, therefore, there was and could be no activity at all. The misunderstanding arises because we forget, as the process of thinking goes

## MATHEMATICAL THOUGHT AND MECHANISM

on, the abstraction with which we started. And we reach a materialistic and deterministic conclusion precisely because we started by limiting our thought to the consideration of that in the world which is mechanically determined.

This conclusion is very liable to be misunderstood. There is a deal of truth in Bergson's insistence that the function of the intellect is to deal with matter. The method of thought which is most familiar to us, and which we habitually employ, is mathematical in type. Our tendency, if we accept the conclusion, will be to vitiate it by interpreting it in terms of mathematical thought. We will tend to think that some things in the world are mechanically determined while others are not. The vicious dualism between matter and mind is itself the product of a mechanical analysis. *Everything* in the world is material. It may be that nothing in the world is merely material, though certainly much that is in the world is more nearly pure matter than the rest. Even in the field of what we usually call material objects, there seem to be features which escape from the meshes of the mathematical net. But organisms and persons, whatever more they may be, are certainly material objects. It follows that there is nothing in the world as we know it in immediate experience, to which mathematical thought is inapplicable. The proper way to state the limitation of this type of symbolic interpretation is to say that it is valid for reality *in so far as it is material*. It would be wrong to say that it is only valid for material objects. It is, in fact, valid for anything that can be acted upon, or anything that has a material aspect; that can be used as an instrument or be the means to an end. But it is only valid of anything within this limit. So far as anything is more than passive, not merely a means or an instrument, it possesses characteristics which cannot be represented in this symbolism, and which, for that reason, cannot be dealt with by the activities of mathematical thought. The limits of mathematical thought are, in fact, the limits of science. Science cannot offer us and should not be expected to offer us an interpretation of the universe. It is limited by the abstraction which creates it, and to apply its results beyond these limits is merely to be unscientific and illogical.

## FIVE

# Biological Thought and Organism

The second unity-pattern which calls for consideration is the one we employ for the representation of life and the processes in which life consists. We must begin by recognizing that it is impossible to pass directly from mathematical thought to a representation of the organic. Our understanding of the world in so far as it is material depends upon the use of a particular method of reproducing in imagination the unity that is given in our immediate experience of matter. We have seen that this involves an atomic analysis of the object to adapt it to the formula of construction which lies at the basis of mathematical thinking. However far we carry our mathematical thought it still depends throughout upon the unity-pattern which guides it, and as that pattern exists for the purpose of representing the world as material, any understanding which it achieves is necessarily an understanding of things in so far as they are material, and not an understanding of them in so far as they are alive. If what we wish to represent is the world in so far as it is organic, we shall have to employ from the beginning a unity-pattern of a different kind. In the nature of things, no reflection upon our experience of matter and no reflection upon mathematical thought or its methods and conclusions can provide us with the unity-pattern which we need. We must return to our immediate experience of life and discover, through a reflection upon that, the kind of representation of unity in idea which will enable us to express the unity of life as we know it.

# BIOLOGICAL THOUGHT AND ORGANISM

There is a sense in which all our thinking is necessarily anthropomorphic. Our consciousness of the world is equally a consciousness of ourselves. If it were not, reflection would be impossible. This is a point which both modern philosophy and modern psychology have established in their different fashions. But beyond this lies a further truth. The way in which we apprehend the world determines the way in which we apprehend ourselves. Our apprehension of matter is, on the subjective side, an apprehension of ourselves as material bodies, while our apprehension of ourselves as living organisms is the inner aspect of our apprehension of life in the world. Nor can we know ourselves as persons except in the knowledge of persons who are not ourselves. I am speaking here of our immediate experience, not of our reflective understanding. It is quite possible to think of ourselves in terms which are only adequate to describe the world in so far as it is material. But this is only possible because we already know ourselves, in our knowledge of other selves, as persons. And the representation of ourselves as persons in materialistic terms will, of course, be inadequate to our immediate knowledge of personality.

Philosophers have often discussed how we come to know that other persons exist, and they have discussed it on the assumption that we apprehend other persons as material objects, and go on to infer that they are alive and that they are rational because of the similarity of their appearance and their movements to our own. This is to assume that we can infer from a material representation to the existence of life. Such an inference must be illicit. If we did not already know that they were alive we should not know that there was such a thing as life. Our immediate knowledge of life in the world is the basis, and the only possible basis, for determining, by thought, that certain objects in the world are alive. We know that other living creatures exist because we know other living creatures. We know that other persons exist because we know other persons. We have an immediate experience of life upon which any representation of the characteristics of life in reflective thought must be based. Indeed, our immediate

## BIOLOGICAL THOUGHT AND ORGANISM

knowledge of life is prior to our immediate knowledge of matter. Children would seem to begin with the assumption that material objects are alive, and to learn that they are not.

Our immediate knowledge of life is different in type from our immediate knowledge of matter. Perhaps it would be truer to say that it is on a higher level; because, while it involves all the avenues of consciousness which yield us an apprehension of the world as material, it calls into play also new aspects and capacities of consciousness which matter fails to awaken. We can be conscious of matter without being conscious of the life in our own bodies. We cannot be conscious of living creatures in this way. They awaken in us the consciousness of organic processes in ourselves which are harmonious with, and correspond to, processes of life in themselves. Such a consciousness of life involves feeling as well as sense-perception, the type of feeling which makes us aware of the organic processes in our own bodies. It is, of course, possible to contemplate an animal without having such feelings aroused But when this occurs we are aware of it not as an animal but only in so far as it is a material object. We know that it is an animal and alive, but we are not aware of it as an animal, nor of its life. Even this knowledge that it is alive rests upon the immediate apprehension of life through feeling on other occasions. The contrast between these two modes of consciousness is not one that we need develop here. One very interesting account of it is to be found in Schopenhauer's magnum opus *The World as Will and Idea*, where the distinction between idea and feeling is made the basis of a complete philosophical system.

When we return to our immediate experience of life we find, in the first place, that we are dealing with material objects which manifest characteristics of a new kind. The most important of these is the activity of growth. By this we do not mean merely an increase in size, but an increase in differentiation and co-ordination of their parts through a time-process. The problem which this presents to reflection is a new one and quite different from the problem set by matter. In the case of matter it is possible to represent change as a rearrangement of elements which do not

## BIOLOGICAL THOUGHT AND ORGANISM

themselves change. In the case of an object which grows this is not possible, because the changes which constitute its growth are essential to its being what it is. We shall obviously misrepresent growth if we represent it merely as an accident that happens to the organism, since in the absence of growth it would not be alive. But, further, growth involves the development of differentiation, and, therefore, the differences between the elements which constitute it are essential in the description of a living creature. We cannot represent these elements as identical. Lastly, the differentiation of its parts has to be of such a nature that the unity of the whole remains unimpaired, and for this the differences must be complementary and harmonious. In terms of growth and of the maintenance of life, this means that the differentiation of its elements is really a differentiation of their functions in maintaining the developing unity of the whole. It is these characteristics of the living thing which must be represented in the unity-pattern which reflection uses for the analysis and understanding of life, and they are such that none of them can be represented by the mechanical unity-pattern of mathematical thought.

Let us consider first what is sometimes called the material basis of life, by which is meant the arrangement of the elements in a living creature so far as it is material. We should note in passing that this involves disregarding for the moment the essential fact that life is a process of development. We take the living creature at one moment, and consider it as it is at that moment. In fact, life never *is* at any moment. It is always *becoming*. We often talk as if the material of which a living body is composed were preserved throughout its life. Yet life is essentially, so far as it is material, a process of metabolism. It consists in getting rid of the material of which the body is composed, and replacing it continuously by new material, not exactly but with variations. The matter of the living body is not preserved. It is in a continual process of dissolution and replacement. The form is preserved, but again not exactly, but with variations.

If we abstract from its growth, and take a cross-section, as it were, of the life of the organism at a particular moment, we find

## BIOLOGICAL THOUGHT AND ORGANISM

that it consists of a set of parts or elements which differ from one another. These differences are so arranged that they preserve a form. This general characteristic dictates the first characteristic of the unity-pattern that reflection requires. We must represent the unity of what is alive as a unity of differences, not as a unity of identities. It follows that the organic whole cannot be represented as the sum of its parts. You cannot sum differences. How, then, can the unity of differences be represented?

It can be represented only in æsthetic terms, as a balance or harmony. The work of a painter, for example, consists, in part at least, in combining different colours harmoniously so that they can produce an effect of unity. A work of art is always a unity of differences and that is why we often speak of it as an *organic* unity. Such a unity is felt, not calculated. It may seem that this is a drawback from the point of view of reflective thought. It is, in fact, only a drawback from the standpoint of mathematical thought, or from the standpoint of the logical intellect which wishes to perform its tricks in isolation from the other capacities of consciousness. Life itself is apprehended in immediate experience only through a co-operation of sense and feeling. We need not be surprised to find that the reflective representation of life involves the co-operation of feeling for harmony, rhythm and balance, with the ordinary processes of intellectual activity. Apart from this, the representation of life in symbolic form is just impossible.

The living thing, then, must be represented as a harmony of differences to form a unity. This, however, ignores the essential processes of growth. These must also be represented, if we are to think of life at all. This can be achieved by representing the different elements in the unity as themselves in process, and these processes of the different elements as themselves harmoniously combined to form a unity of processes which is the life of the organism as a whole. Each of these processes which are elements in the life-process of the individual organism will be represented as a function of the whole process. We shall say that each different element in the living creature has a function to perform in the whole, for the whole. We shall recognize that the differences of the

## BIOLOGICAL THOUGHT AND ORGANISM

material elements in the organism are determined by and relative to the differences in the function which each has to perform in the life of the organism. Form, we shall say, is relative to function, and the unity of the organism is a unity of functions.

There is still a third element which demands representation in the unity-pattern before it can be complete. It is the fact of development. It would be quite possible to imagine a unity of functions which should be purely cyclical, in which a cycle of interrelated activities repeated itself mechanically *ad infinitum*. But life, as we know it, is not merely this. It involves development in time as well as the repetition of processes. It involves this not merely relatively, within the life of the individual, but also absolutely, in the development of species, which is nothing but the extension of growth beyond the life of individual organisms through the processes of reproduction. Growth can perhaps be defined as reproduction with variation, even within the life of the individual, but that is a point which we need not consider here.

If we consider any finite process of development we notice that it has to be completed before we can apprehend it as a whole. Its beginning does not reveal its full nature. We do not know the nature of a seed until we know the full-grown plant from which it is derived and into which it will itself develop. To understand a process of development it is necessary to know its final state, or at least its state of complete development. Earlier stages are only stages in the process because they lead to a mature state. An organism can be defined only in terms of its maturity, and its growth only as the series of forms which it takes on in its progress to maturity. For this reason the representation of life must be teleological. The life of an organism can only be described and understood by reference to the final state of its natural development.

The conception of teleology is, therefore, an essential element in the unity-pattern by means of which life can be described and understood. There is, however, so much misunderstanding of teleology abroad that we must attempt to define it more closely. In the first place, we must notice that the conception of teleology is merely a way of describing natural processes of growth. It is, indeed, the only possible way. It is not in any sense an explanation of growth but merely the way of representing it symbolically. It does not involve any conception of conscious purpose, or, indeed, of consciousness in any form. To describe a process of growth you must represent the process as governed by the final stage in which it completes itself. We need not, and should not, imply either that the complete stage is present in the earlier stages or that in any sense the growing organism is aware of the final stage before it reaches it. We need not imply that anything or anyone at all is aware of the final stage before it is reached. Given the complete process, we analyse it into a series of stages which succeed one another in time. We note that each stage is necessarily different from every other. If this is all we notice, however, we have not really described the process as a process of *growth*. We have omitted to notice that what is essential to each stage is that it develops into the next by its very nature, and cannot develop into any other; nor can there be a development from the first stage to the last which does not pass through all the intervening stages. To express this we need the idea of potentiality. Any stage in a process of growth has the potentiality of developing into the next. This potentiality is not an element in its make-up. It is merely the fact that it will give place to the next under appropriate conditions and that it is its nature to do so. This simple way of describing the fact of growth is often confused with the idea of purpose. We are familiar with the processes by which we achieve results which we consciously desire, by taking the appropriate steps to produce them. The process of realizing a purpose is not, however, a process of growth. It is a process of deliberate and conscious activity. To call such activity teleological is to use the term in a different sense, which offers our desire for the end as the *explanation* why a certain course of action was undertaken. The teleological description of the process of growth is not offered as an explanation of why the growth takes place, but merely as a description of the fact. In no sense does organic teleology imply purpose or even purposiveness.

We have now determined the unity-pattern which underlies

## BIOLOGICAL THOUGHT AND ORGANISM

organic thought. It is the conception of the organism as a whole, whose unity is maintained by the harmony of differences, and in which the differences are finally differences of function in a unitary process in which the potentiality of the beginning is realized in the end. It would be too complicated a task to go on to define the laws of construction which govern the thought which is based upon the development of this unity-pattern. The task was undertaken and carried through successfully by Hegel in his *Logic*. Organic thought is essentially dialectical. It proceeds by the generation of opposites which are unified in a synthesis that overcomes their opposition by creating a harmony of their differences and so exhibiting them as functional differentiations of a developing unity. Modern idealist philosophy uses this biological type of thought for interpreting the universe. Modern realism, too, when it is not merely a recoil from the defects of the organic conception into mathematical thought once more, is equally an organic realism resting upon the unity-pattern of biological thought.

It is to the limitations of biological thought and so to its defects as a representation of the universe as a whole that we must now turn our attention. We should notice, in the first place, that this unity-pattern may be misused, and that its misuse is not a defect in *it*. It is misused when it is employed as a substitute for mathematical thought, to interpret anything so far as it is material. Now, since every organism is also a material object the interpretation of how it works, as distinct from the expression of its behaviour as a growing unity, is properly mechanical. All enquiries of a scientific kind about life, seeing that they are inquiries into the working of the organism, will rightly proceed in terms of mathematical thought. Such enquiries will fall within the unity-pattern of organic thought and presuppose it. This corresponds to the fact that our consciousness of life includes our consciousness of material objects, and raises it to a higher level by awakening the feeling through which, as we have seen, life is immediately apprehended. In reflection the conception of the organism rests upon the apprehension of harmony in difference, which is essentially an apprehension not of a scientific but of an æsthetic character. In the activity of reflection upon life the æsthetic apprehension of harmony forms a framework within which the intellectual activities of mathematical or scientific thought must work. It will define, as it were, a new form within which the mechanical form must fall.

The significance of the last paragraph lies in its bearing upon the controversy over vitalism in biology, since it implies neither the vitalist nor the mechanistic position, but the view that the controversy itself is misconceived. Vitalism in its usual form is merely a mystical mechanism which conceives the life-principle as another element within the unity-pattern of mathematical thought. Scientific biology cannot admit such a vitalism because it vitiates its unity-pattern. So far the mechanist in biology is correct. Vitalism is an attempt to represent the mechanical processes of life in so far as they are material, as if they at once were and were not mechanical processes. On the other hand, the mechanist, if he offers to answer the question about the nature of life in mechanical terms, is implying that a living organism is not alive, and so denying the existence of the problem which he proposes to solve. To that extent the vitalist is right in objecting that life cannot be defined in material terms. What needs to be recognized is that biological science, just because it is a scientific enquiry, must be mathematical in type, but that for this reason it cannot be an attempt to define the nature of life but only an effort to represent and understand the mechanism through which life works. The possibility of scientific biology of a mechanistic character depends upon the recognition—which is always vaguely present to the biologist's mind and ought always to be consciously and clearly recognized—of the organism as a harmony of functional differences circumscribing and so determining the form within which the mechanical processes which he investigates take place, and which gives them their specific significance as processes of life.

With this difficulty removed we may consider whether the organic unity-pattern can properly be used as the basis of a philosophical interpretation of the universe. Perhaps the simplest way of stating this question is to ask, 'Is the universe an organic whole?' Modern idealism answers this question in the affirmative. But in doing so it is apt to offer the organic type of interpretation as a substitute for thought of the mathematical type and so to misuse the organic unity-pattern. In doing so it claims implicitly, and sometimes explicitly, to supersede mathematical thought and science. The difficulty which then faces it is this, that if the universe is an organism there can be no organisms in it, for the different elements in the organic unity-pattern cannot themselves be organic wholes. They must be merely differentiated functions of the organic whole. The whole is either not an individual at all or else the only individual. On the other hand, a modern realism—like the philosophy of Professor Alexander, for example—does involve a true understanding of the way in which the unity-pattern of biological thought can be applied to the interpretation of the world. It represents the mathematical structure of the universe as falling within and providing the basis for its structure as an evolutionary development.

But now, even if it is properly applied, the organic form including the mechanical form within it, the unity-pattern is inadequate to represent the universe as we know it in immediate experience. In the first place, we have to notice the limitation of teleology. Its use depends upon the representation of a stage at which growth is complete, and unless this stage is represented the process of life cannot be defined. The earlier stages are all relative to the stage of maturity. Now our immediate apprehension of life is the apprehension of the infinity of life in finite individuals and, therefore, the process of life is *known* as an infinite process, that is to say, as a process which has no final stage. It follows from this that it is impossible to represent the unity of the world which is given in immediate experience in terms of the organic unity-pattern. Just as in the case of mechanical thought, this type of symbolism must be limited to the interpretation of the finite. It can represent the final life-processes of individual organisms or of species or even of the whole process of evolution up to date, provided that we take the appearance of rational consciousness in humanity as

## BIOLOGICAL THOUGHT AND ORGANISM

the final stage. Beyond this it cannot go, and yet in its very nature it demands that all stages shall be represented as transitions to a more highly developed stage.

In the second place, the conception of the finite organism is meaningless except in relation to the conception of its environment. Here is another point in which we find the demand for something beyond the organism, in terms of which it can be an organism. The moment we begin to apply the unity-pattern to the world as we know it, we discover that we cannot understand the living creature in terms of itself. Its life, and hence its growth, though it is essential to its own nature, though it is, that is to say, an inner spontaneity and not the effect of an impressed force, is nevertheless conditioned by its environment and proceeds as an adaptation to the environment and as a response to the stimulus which the environment alone can provide. It follows once again that such a symbolism cannot be applied to the universe as a whole, since, if it were, the universe would need an environment to provide the stimulus to which its evolution could be the response. And the universe, by definition, can have no environment.

We see, then, that the effort to represent the universe as an organic whole must fail. The symbolism is inherently inadequate to the purpose for which it is used. Philosophical thought cannot be successful if it bases itself upon the unity-pattern of biological thought, however accurately it understands and applies its symbolism. The concrete point in our immediate experience of the world, at which the difficulty is brought into clear focus, is our experience of human personality. It may be possible to represent subjective and irrational forms of consciousness in terms of the biological unity-pattern. But it is certainly not possible to represent the nature of rational or objective consciousness as we know it in immediate experience through this form of symbolism. Human consciousness is not organic. When we return to consider this aspect of our immediate experience of the world, we discover the need for another and more adequate form of symbolism to describe and express what we know.

## SIX

# Psychological Thought and Personality

The failure of mathematical thought drove us back to immediate experience. The failure of biological thought does the same, and for the same reason. The unity-pattern on which it works demands something beyond itself, something which we know but which biological thought does not symbolize. This something beyond is our immediate experience of persons. That persons are apprehended as organisms and something more is, indeed, obvious. And it is this something more that lies beyond the organic unity-pattern.

But at this point we are in a special difficulty. The unity-patterns of mathematical and of organic thought have already been worked out in the history of philosophy. The unity-pattern through which personality could be represented has not. The problem of the logical representation of the self has, indeed, been the central problem of all modern philosophy. The Cartesians tried to represent the self as a substance and, therefore, in terms of the schema of mathematical thought. The second period, which begins from Kant, having discovered the futility of this attempt, sought to interpret the self as an organism, and so in terms of biological thought. We stand to-day at the point where the failure of this effort has become evident, partly through the realists' criticism of idealist philosophy and partly through the development of scientific psychology. But, so far, all that has come to light is the necessity of a new unity-pattern which will be capable of overcoming the limitations of the earlier forms of symbolism. No one has yet produced the pattern of thought that we need. All that we can do, therefore, is to discover, through reflection upon our empirical experience of the personal, the main characteristics which differentiate it from the material and the organic, and which will require to be represented in any unity-pattern that is to be adequate for our purpose.

We may remind ourselves, to start with, that the unity of immediate experience consists in the apprehension of the infinite in the finite, and that the unity-pattern of reflective thought is an attempt to express this unity as a form of synthesis, that is to say, as a way in which the elements which are isolated by reflective analysis can be built together in imagination to form a whole. This general principle we have to apply to our experience of persons. The unity of personality, as we know it in the immediacy of living, is an apprehension of infinite personality in finite persons. We find ourselves, therefore, as analogy would lead us to expect, in the field of religion. 'God' is the term which symbolizes the infinite apprehended as personal, and it derives, as indeed it must, from our immediate experience of the infinite in finite persons. The idea of incarnation, which in one form or other appears in all immediate religions, merely expresses the fact that our awareness of the personal infinite comes to us, and can only come, in and through our awareness of finite personality.

This, however, though it provides the milieu, as it were, within which our researches must proceed, does not take us very far. For, until we have discovered how to symbolize our experience of persons as persons, our thinking is bound to misrepresent the nature of finite and of infinite personality alike. The question which faces us is simply 'What is the essential nature of personality as we know it in immediate experience?'

It is only when we reflect upon our experience of persons that we ourselves, including our activity of reflection, come into the picture. So long as we are reflecting upon matter or life, we ourselves, as persons, stand outside the aspect of reality upon which our thought is directed. But now our reflection places us

# PSYCHOLOGICAL THOUGHT AND PERSONALITY

within the world about which we are thinking. Our thought is, for the first time, about ourselves.

This does not mean, however, that we are now thinking about ourselves in distinction from everything else. It is only accidentally that we, the thinkers, are included. Reflection upon personality, like all forms of reflection, arises from some opposition that we meet in the full practical experience of life. It will take the form of reflection upon personality where the obstacle that brings action to a stop and forces us to think is directly concerned with persons in their nature as persons. In other words, it is when 'we cannot get on with people', as we say, that we stop to think about them. It is from our need to understand other persons that our reflection upon personality arises. How, then, we may ask, does it come about that such reflection immediately forces us to include ourselves?

It is partly the inherent correlation between our consciousness of self and of not-self to which I drew attention in the last chapter. Our awareness of other persons as persons awakens a complete consciousness in ourselves, so that we function fully as persons, and so are capable of a full consciousness of ourselves. But this is not all. The experience of other persons has an essential quality which makes it different from any other kind of experience. It is the consciousness of mutual relationship, of the meeting of like with like, for in it we find a response from the object at our own level. It is this essential mutuality which forms the essence of our experience of persons. We know persons, in fact, only by entering into personal relationship with them as equals. In other cases we are always dealing with that which we know to be less than ourselves. For that reason the object is always recognized as in some sense purely for our use or for our enjoyment. It is, of course, possible to treat persons in this way. But it is not possible to do so without making a personal relationship with them impossible, because it involves treating them, at least for the time being, as less than persons. The demand for equality and the assertion of the rights of man by the depressed classes is really an expression of this. It rests upon the recognition that whenever one person treats another as an instrument for his use, or as an object for his enjoyment, he denies in practice—which is more important than theory—the other's essential nature as a person.

This fact places us in the world we are thinking about when we reflect upon personality. In thinking about any but the personal aspect of reality we can abstract from the relationship in which we stand to the object of our thought. We can drop the relationship out of consciousness and consider that aspect of the world as if we stood outside it and it formed a closed system. With persons we cannot do this because our relation to them is essential to the situation upon which we are reflecting. It is this fact that I wish to express when I say that personality is essentially mutual; that it exists only in and through personal relationships.

The traditional definition of humanity is that man is a rational animal. This, however, is merely a verbal definition until we have defined what we mean by rationality. The question becomes 'What is reason as we know it in immediate experience?' A very natural answer to this question is that reason is the capacity to think. I am afraid it is a bad answer. Thinking, in that sense, means thinking rationally, and the explanation is tautologous. From the psychologist's point of view, thinking is as often as not quite irrational, so that the question 'When is thought rational?'—the question that logic tries to answer—is really part of the question 'What is reason?' I venture, therefore, to offer another definition, that reason is the capacity for objectivity, and to say that it is the possession of this capacity which distinguishes persons from whatever is sub-personal.

By the capacity for objectivity, I mean the capacity to stand in conscious relation to that which is recognized as not ourselves. Everything, of course, stands in relation to what is not itself, and everything that is capable of consciousness stands in conscious relation to what is not itself. This, however, is not sufficient to constitute rationality. We must add that that to which we stand in conscious relation is recognized, is consciously apprehended, as not ourselves. The difficulty of expressing this fact in words arises because it is the very essence of our experience as persons, and so is all-pervasive. To express it clearly it would be necessary

# PSYCHOLOGICAL THOUGHT AND PERSONALITY

to contrast it with a type of consciousness from which objectivity is absent, that is to say, with a purely subjective consciousness. Dream-consciousness is probably as near as most of us can get to this, though even our dreams have an objectivity about them which is reflected from our waking experience. Certain abnormal states of consciousness bring us even nearer to the representation of a purely subjective consciousness, and it is largely through the researches of modern psychologists and especially through the technique developed by medical psychologists for the analysis of abnormal psychical conditions that we are beginning to discover the nature of subjectivity, that is to say, of a consciousness deprived of rationality. Let us try to use the more familiar contrast between dreams and waking experience to get at the nature of objectivity.

A dentist whose hobby it was to collect the dreams which his patients had under gas relates one which has always struck me as of peculiar interest. His patient was having a tooth extracted, and when the operation was over and the man had recovered consciousness, the dentist asked him whether he had had a dream. He replied that he dreamed that he was cycling down a very steep, straight hill and that he lost control of his bicycle. It was all he could do to keep it in the middle of the road. Suddenly he noticed that lower down two huge rocks, jutting out from either side of the road, left only a narrow passage through which he must try to steer his bicycle. He wondered anxiously whether he could manage it. Just as he came to the rocks he heard a loud voice shouting from the other side, 'You're too stout! You're too stout! You're too stout!' When he had heard the dream, the dentist smiled and replied, 'Do you know what you really heard? I was trying to wake you up, and kept shouting at you, "Your tooth's out! Your tooth's out!"' There are several points of interest in this dream, but what we are concerned with is the contrast which it illustrates, up to a point, between subjectivity and objectivity. There is an actual relationship between the dentist calling 'Your tooth's out'—which is the real situation—and the dream experience which the patient had. The dream is a

## PSYCHOLOGICAL THOUGHT AND PERSONALITY

response in consciousness to the actual situation. But it is not, in any sense, a recognition of the actual situation. It is a subjective misinterpretation of the real state of affairs. The moment that the patient wakes up he no longer has merely a conscious reaction to the situation but an objective awareness of it. He was conscious in the dream. He is conscious when he wakes up. But there is a difference. When he is awake he is conscious of what is there outside himself. In the dream he was not. His dream-consciousness was merely a response to the stimulus provided by the real situation.

This is, perhaps, the simplest way of expressing the difference between subjective and objective consciousness. We have the same two factors in both cases. On the one hand we have the subject with the capacity of consciousness; on the other we have an external world to which the subject stands in relation. Through the co-operation of these two factors the conscious experience is generated. But now comes the difference. In the one case the dream-content is a response or adaptation to the stimulus of the environment. In the other case the content of consciousness—the phrase is a bad one, though it is often used—is knowledge, that is to say, it is an awareness *of* the environment, not a response *to* it. Thus, an objective consciousness or a rational consciousness—the two phrases have the same meaning—is a consciousness of what is recognized in the consciousness itself as an object independent of the subject.

Now objectivity or reason, which is the essential characteristic of personal consciousness, is not confined to any one aspect of consciousness. It is the essence of personal consciousness as such. Rationality is not a peculiar characteristic of the intellect. It is equally characteristic of the emotional life. We can put this in terms of the expressions of personality by saying that art and religion are just as rational as science or philosophy. The rationality of thought does not lie in the thought itself, as a quality of it, but depends upon its reference to the external world as known in immediate experience. As we have seen already, thought as an activity of the mind is an activity of the imagina-

## PSYCHOLOGICAL THOUGHT AND PERSONALITY

tion. What makes it rational or logical is the purpose which governs it—the purpose of expressing symbolically some aspect of the world we know. Our emotions have this same characteristic of referring to that which is recognized as not ourselves. That they are often subjective is beyond doubt; but then, so are our thoughts. We recognize that thought may be false as well as true and that only when it is true is it appropriately related to the world to which it refers. Equally, we recognize that our feelings and emotions refer to real things and that they may be appropriate or inappropriate to the situation to which they refer. I may feel angry with someone and recognize at the same time that I have no reason to feel angry. In that case I recognize that my anger is unreasonable. In recognizing *that*, I recognize that my emotions are capable of exhibiting the quality of reason, that they may or may not fit the objective world to which they consciously refer.

We must remember that in the full, concrete activity of personal life the various aspects of our consciousness are not separate, but fused in the experience of spontaneous activity. It follows that objectivity or rationality expresses itself concretely only as a rationality or objectivity of living in which reasonableness of thought and of emotion are merely aspects. Personality is an essential objectivity of conscious living. Such an objectivity is not usually attained in actual human experience, in spite of the fact that human experience can only be defined in terms of it. There are, in fact, two ways in which we fall short of our essential nature. Our rationality may be falsified or it may be incompletely expressed. It is falsified when we take as objective a conscious experience of our own which is, in fact, subjective. We are then in error. A false judgment, for example, is a thought. It is an element in our conscious experience. But it is only false if we take it to reveal the nature of the objective world. We cannot at once be in error and know that we are in error. On the other hand, we may be partially rational without being in error. We may, for example, indulge in subjective experience knowing that it is subjective, as when we give ourselves over to pure daydreaming or to the play of fancy for its own sake. But, more importantly, we may limit our experience to aspects of itself which fail to bring out the full capacity of reason in us. We may limit ourselves to the experience of matter and its control. If we do so, as a general principle, we devote our lives to the pursuit of power and, in reflection, to the development of science. Or we may limit our rationality to the organic field, in which case our lives will be devoted to achieving an individual fineness of living and, in reflection, to the development of art. In both these cases there is a limitation of rationality. Only part of our capacity for objectivity is called into exercise. There remains always an aspect of the world to which we are only subjectively related. Complete objectivity depends upon our being objectively related, in action as well as in reflection, to that in the world which is capable of calling into play all the capacities of our consciousness at once. It is only the personal aspect of the world that can do this, and, therefore, it is only the objectivity of our conscious relation to other persons which can express our rationality fully and so reveal its essential character.

The key to the nature of personality, and so of reason, lies, then, in the nature of inter-personal consciousness, or, in plain terms, in the nature of friendship. Friendship is the name that we give to such relationships between persons as are fully personal, that is to say, in which one person is consciously related to another as a person in terms of his personality. Two persons, may, of course, be in conscious relation without being friends. They may co-operate for the achievement of a common purpose. In that case, the relationship is not personal but functional and teleological, and so, of the organic type. It can be described completely in terms of the unity-pattern of organic thought. It calls into play less than the full capacity for human relationship between the persons concerned. A personal relationship is one in which individuals are related as persons, not as complementary functions in an organic process, still less as the instrument and its employer, as is the case of master and servant. It is only when the relationship is one of friendship—or of its negative, enmity— that the relation is a personal one. And it is only in the objectivity

## PSYCHOLOGICAL THOUGHT AND PERSONALITY

of such a relationship that complete rationality can be achieved or expressed.

It does not follow that in such relationships complete rationality *will* be achieved or expressed. Indeed, the difficulty of achievement will here be at its greatest. To limit the field in which rationality seeks expression makes the task of achieving objectivity a simpler one, and the greater the limitation the easier will be the task. That is why it is so much easier to point to examples of obvious rationality in the intellectual field. Science is far easier than art, and art again is far easier than religion, the field of which is the field of personal relationship. In every field the danger of being in error, that is, of falling into subjectivity of which we are unaware, is continuously present.

If we wish to discover, then, the new elements which have to be represented in the description of personality, and so in the unity-pattern of psychological thought, we have to reflect upon the nature of personal relationships in their completely personal character. The success of such reflection will determine the form of personal thought, within which the forms of thought which we have already discussed must fall. The main characteristic which reflection reveals is the mutuality of the conscious relationship. Only in a fully personal relationship with another person do I find a response at my own level. My own objectivity meets an objectivity which corresponds to it, so that for the first time I can achieve self-consciousness. My self-consciousness is my consciousness of myself as a person, and it is only possible in and through my consciousness of a person who is not myself. It is only in personal relationships that I can be conscious of personality. The basic fact about human beings, in virtue of which they are human, is that they know one another and live in that knowledge. On this, everything else hinges. If this is denied, explicitly or implicitly, then everything is denied, including rationality.

We can go a step further. A person is a self-conscious being. If he were not self-conscious he would not be a person. In other words, personality not merely *implies* but *is constituted by* self-consciousness. Now, if self-consciousness is merely the inner

## PSYCHOLOGICAL THOUGHT AND PERSONALITY

aspect of our consciousness of other persons, it follows that personality is constituted by, and does not merely imply, personal relationships between persons. Personality is mutual in its very being. The self is one term in a relation between two selves. It cannot be prior to that relation and equally, of course, the relation cannot be prior to it. '*I*' exist only as one member of the '*you and I*'. The self only exists in the communion of selves.

We must beware of misrepresenting this statement by forgetting that the self is a self. It is the subject of experience, not the object or part of the object. There are plenty of terms which exist only in relation to other terms. But those terms and the relations which constitute them are objects for objective consciousness. My own existence as a person is constituted by my *knowledge* of other persons, by my objective consciousness of them as persons, not by the mere fact of my relation to them. The main fact that has to be represented is not that I am because you are, but that I am I because I know you, and that you are you because you know me. My consciousness is rational or objective because it is a consciousness of someone who is in personal relation to me and, therefore, knows me and knows that I am I. I have my being in that mutual self-knowledge.

Into this personal being all my other knowledge and all that I experience is taken up. The personal experience, though it is essentially an experience of persons, yet includes all other possible experience. It is only through it that I can be rational at all and, therefore, know the world in any of its aspects. In other words, the community of conscious beings, which is what I experience in personal relationships, is the experience of a personal world which is all-inclusive of all experience. This point brings us back to where we started. The immediate experience of personality is the experience of infinite personality in finite persons, and so it is the experience of God as the personal absolute, as the unity of persons in relationship; it is the knowledge of that personality 'in whom we live and move and have our being', as St. Paul put it long ago. But the analysis of all that is implied in this would take us far beyond the modest scope of this chapter.

## PSYCHOLOGICAL THOUGHT AND PERSONALITY

All that we can do is to state the problem which our immediate experience of personality sets for reflective thought. How are we to represent the type of unity which we know in our experience of the personal? A person cannot be represented as a mathematical unit because, though each person can say of himself '*I am I*', no person can say of any other '*I am I*' or '*I am you*', but only '*you are you and not I*'. And apart from this difference of *I* and *you*, there would be neither the one nor the other. The units of material existence are bare identities. One unit is identical with every other and its equivalent. Thus, two mathematical units have no real otherness between them. In the case of two persons, both are individuals, yet their otherness is essential to their individuality. For each of us, there can be only one '*I*'. The other person is always '*you*'. Yet it is equally essential to my being that in knowing you I know that for yourself you are '*I*' and for you I am the other, the '*you*'. This can obviously not be represented by mathematical thought, for which all units are equally '*it*'. The difference between *I* and *you* must be represented in any symbolism which is to be of use in formulating our experience of the personal.

Organic thought, as we saw, does involve the representation of the essential differences between elements in the whole. But this expression of difference is in terms of complementary functions, so that no element in an organic whole can be really individual. Only the whole can possess true individuality. For this reason organic thought, in its turn, cannot express the nature of the personal. For the personal involves the essential individuality of all persons as well as their differences. Two persons in personal relation are not complementary. They do not lose their individuality to become functional elements in an individuality which includes them both. In fact, in the personal field the only real individuals are individual persons. Groups of persons are not individuals. Nevertheless, the individuality of a person exists only in and through his relationship to other persons and the more objective his relations become with other persons, the more his individuality is enhanced. It would seem, therefore, that the

## PSYCHOLOGICAL THOUGHT AND PERSONALITY

unity-pattern of psychological thought must somehow succeed in combining the characteristics both of organic and of mathematical thought. It must express at once the independent reality of the individual and the fact that this individuality is constituted by the relationship in which he stands to other independent persons who are different individuals. To put it in the familiar terms of modern controversy, mathematical relations are external to the terms they relate. Organic relations are internal to their terms. But personal relations are at once internal and external. They create not merely a unity between individuals, but also the difference of the individuals which they unite. Further than this we are not in a position to go. Any further advance would involve the solution of the problem which is emerging in our own time as the central problem of contemporary philosophy.

SEVEN

# Logic and Life

The course of the argument has brought us to a point at which we are faced with a logical problem which is unsolved, and which we are unable to solve. We do not know how to represent our knowledge of the personal in idea. I have indicated my belief that this is the emergent problem of philosophy in our own day. We are discovering that we do not understand personality, that we cannot express in reflection our immediate knowledge of persons. That, in itself, is not enough to constitute a real philosophical question. There must be, in addition, a real need to understand, forced upon us by the conditions of our immediate life. Only when the need for understanding is forced upon us by life itself does any problem become of more than academic interest. We must conclude our study by asking why this problem emerges in our own day, and why it is necessary for philosophy to attempt its solution.

The theory of knowledge which has been outlined in earlier chapters is radically different from traditional theory because it insists upon relating the activities of thought to the wider activity of life itself. It has demanded a reason for reflection as well as rationality in reflection. It has insisted that knowledge is prior to thought and that thought itself is the specialization of imagination to meet a practical need. If this is so, the rationality of thought is derivative. Thought is functional, and is of value only when it fulfils its function in the economy of life. It is not and

## LOGIC AND LIFE

cannot be self-sufficient. Life is wider than logic and logic must be justified in terms of life. The theoretical difficulties which such a view may seem to raise depend upon the false belief that thought is prior to knowledge. It is only when thought is regarded as the sole avenue to knowledge that 'the scepticism of the instrument' need result in despair. If thought is itself surrounded and supported by a knowledge which it does not produce, it can be shaped and tested by that knowledge.

Human life has its own evolution, which is expressed in the movement of history. The development of thought is merely an aspect of this evolution, and the deliberate development of knowledge by means of thought is a very late product of the movement of history. It is, indeed, only during the last few centuries that thought has become of outstanding importance in the process of human evolution. But in that short period the effort of sustained, deliberate and systematic thinking, which has discovered a method of relating itself to the immediacy of practical life and of testing and reshaping its results by reference to practical activity, has succeeded in changing radically and with increasing rapidity the conditions under which human life is lived. During the last few centuries men have been awakening to the potentiality of thought as a means for controlling their environment, and discovering the conditions under which this potentiality could be utilized. Thought has become a necessity and not a luxury.

The discovery of the conditions under which thought could become the instrument for the control of the environment has been gradual, for it has itself been the result of the effort to use thought as an instrument of control. The changes which it worked have themselves brought to light new problems to be solved and made the solution of them essential to further progress. Once this process has been started, it must go on, on penalty of a relapse into primitive conditions and the loss of the progress in civilization which has been brought about by the partial control already achieved. Civilization has reached the stage, in our own day, when we are all aware that a new and more strenuous effort of thought is necessary to preserve it. To maintain the control

## LOGIC AND LIFE

over nature which we have achieved, we must increase that control and extend it over new fields. We have, in fact, reached the point at which the understanding of personality is essential to the control of material conditions. To understand this we must cast a glance over the historical development of science in order to see how the problem of mechanical thought produced the problem of biological thought and is now forcing the psychological problem upon us.

Before the emergence of science human life was almost completely at the mercy of its environment. In the last resort everything was determined by economic conditions. Man was at the mercy of his organic needs. Here and there, for short periods, small numbers of individuals succeeded in escaping from the pressure of the universal scarcity of food and shelter at the expense of their fellows and so in achieving, for themselves, a precarious control of the conditions of life. But human life as a whole never escaped from the pressure of scarcity, and the movement of history was determined, all but completely, by the economic struggle for the necessities of life. Other factors were present, no doubt, and it is on them that we prefer to dwell when we think of the past. But they were mere eddies on the surface of the main stream.

The development of science has been the first sustained attempt that the human race has made to escape from the clutches of economic necessity. Seen in its relation to history, it is the effort to turn the control of man by the environment into a control of the environment by man. In the Renaissance, we can trace the beginnings of a human self-assertion against the world. We can see humanity shaking itself out of sleep and awakening to the possibility of escaping from the old tradition of submission to fate. This led to a growing preoccupation with the material world, since the control of conditions means first and foremost the power to use the material of the world for human purposes. The condition of such control is understanding. Science arose as the effort to understand the material world in order to dominate and use it.

It was not for a considerable time that the advance of science began to make any notable difference to the human situation. The general theory of the physical sciences had first to be established. Until the methods of mathematical thought had been invented and developed in relation to the practical problems which were to be solved by their help, and until the instruments of experiment had been produced through which the immediate experience of matter could be adapted to the exigencies of mathematical thought, no general theory of matter, and no general understanding of how the material world might be controlled, was possible. It was not until the results of a long effort had been unified by Newton and the hypothesis of universal gravitation established and verified that the results of the inquiry into the nature of the material universe could become a basis for a large-scale effort to control it. But as soon as this stage had been reached, the application of science became an essential feature in European history, and invention based upon science began to transform the conditions of civilized life. Once begun, the process developed with amazing rapidity.

The application of science to the control of conditions, however, raises a new set of problems. It involves social organization. The organization of society is essentially an adaptation to conditions imposed by the environment. When a society begins to alter its environment in the effort to control conditions, a new adaptation becomes inevitable. When the alteration is a continuous process of applying a growing understanding of the material world to the control of the conditions of life, it necessarily involves a progressive adaptation of social organization to a progressive change in conditions. When, therefore, a society undertakes to discover and utilize the means for the control of its environment, it initiates also a process of social development by which its traditional habits of social life are adapted to the conditions which its own effort creates. It is committed to social progress, with all the disruption of traditional forms which this involves. Since invention began to change the conditions of civilized life, we have been committed to discovering the form of social organization which will make possible in practice the control of condi-

## LOGIC AND LIFE

tions which science has made possible in theory. Since the practical problem is the control of the material environment, the social problem remains essentially an economic problem. It is not, however, the old economic problem of making the best of conditions as they are, but the new one of organizing human effort to create the conditions which it desires. It has become an industrial problem, the problem of organizing human industry for the satisfaction of human needs.

The problems of organization for the control of the environment at once become the essential problems of social life. It is this situation which makes the development of biological thought necessary. The ideas of progress, of adaptation to environment, of the functional relationship of individuals in a co-operative task, come into focus. The main business of thought remains unchanged. It is still the task of understanding and controlling matter. But the accomplishment of this task involves something more. It involves the creation of a society functionally organized to provide and utilize the material means for the accomplishment of the task. In this organization of society for industrialism, thought must play its part. It must develop the understanding that is necessary to control the process of social organization and social development. It must envisage society itself as a developing organization which must be understood properly if the control of matter by man is to be realized. Social organization must be controlled if matter is to be controlled. Human life, therefore, must be considered organically and teleologically. The processes of development through functional organization must be studied. Life in its organic aspect must be understood. We have seen, in an earlier chapter, how this is achieved by the creation of a new type of thought which is adapted to the description and interpretation of the processes of growth and development.

This account of the historical forces which made the problem of the organism the central problem of thought during the last century, enables us to understand better why biological symbolism cannot be a substitute for mathematical thought, and why science even in the field of biology must proceed upon the

## LOGIC AND LIFE

principles of mechanism. Science is throughout concerned with the control of the world in so far as it is material and in relation to the development of human life. It is the theoretical instrument for subordinating the material environment to man. The functional organization of human society for industrial purposes is merely the social condition of making this control of matter effective. The human problem which creates biological thought is not directly concerned with the control of matter, but rather with the direction of human effort in such a way that this control can be exercised. The functional organization of society for economic purposes is the social condition without which it is not possible to release man from bondage to his environment and to enable him to dominate and utilize it. Thus it comes about that organic thought defines a thought-form within which mechanical thought must function if the understanding of the world which it achieves is to be utilized. Without the understanding which enables us to direct the course of social evolution towards the goal which is set by the effort to control the material environment, the application of our understanding of matter in mechanical terms could not be accomplished.

During the past century this process of creating a society functionally organized for the control of the material conditions of life has gone on apace in Western Europe. It is not yet complete, but it is sufficiently far advanced to raise problems of a new type which are bound to become increasingly central as its completion draws nearer. The industrialization of society is only a means to an end, and it involves not merely a considerable dislocation of human interests and values, but also a prolonged and concentrated effort in which everyone must share, directed upon the material conditions of life, not upon life itself. The question that is bound to arise is '*Cui bono*? In whose interest is all this expenditure of human energy and all this preoccupation with the environment being undertaken?' The organic answer to this question is that it is undertaken in the interests of society as a whole, that is to say, as an organic whole. Society as a whole, in this sense, is a mere idea unless it means society as organized for the control of the environment. Such an answer begs the question. It implies that the control of the environment is an end in itself, and that it is a matter of no importance which persons in society benefit personally by the activity or, indeed, whether any person benefits at all. It is only possible to disguise this deliberate subordination of life to the conditions of life by projecting the end of the process into the future and conceiving a Utopia of supermen who shall enjoy the fruits of the self-sacrifice of all previous generations. But, from the organic point of view, such a future must lie at an infinite distance; and even if it were realized, it could not be explained in terms of organic thought. The organic answer to the question 'In whose interest?' is merely a way of shelving the question. In practice it cannot be shelved, because the activity itself of organizing society and of controlling the environment through this organization depends upon providing, in the consciousness of all the persons involved in it, a motive and incentive for carrying it on. The activity itself is an activity carried on by persons. It must, therefore, have a personal significance for each of them if the incentive is not to disappear, and the effort with it.

The real answer to this question has two aspects. It will be necessary to justify the effort of functional organization for economic purposes in terms of the advantage, the personal advantage, which it brings to each individual who is required to subordinate himself to it and accept it as his purpose. But since the organization is functional and requires from each individual the willingness to co-operate with all the others for a common purpose, it will require justification also in terms of the personal relationships between the persons who are involved in it. The success of the effort to create a functional economy of society for the control of the conditions of life must necessarily involve the realization of a society of persons living the life of personality in association. It will involve the subordination of the functional economy to the achievement of a community of persons, as persons, to which it is the means.

This problem of subordinating the social control of life through

## LOGIC AND LIFE

economic organization to the human interests of all the individuals concerned is quite obviously the emergent social problem of the contemporary world. The economic organization of society can be carried through in various ways. Some of these ways are already part and parcel of the political effort of our time. We have already communism, fascism and various more or less definite forms of planned economy. They differ in practice by the resultant distribution of the benefits accruing from the social control of economic organization amongst the persons and classes taking part in the effort. They are, whether consciously or unconsciously, different answers to the question 'In whose interest?' They imply an answer to the question of the significance of personal life in society. They are bound, therefore, to bring the problem of the nature of personality into the focus of consciousness. Without an understanding of personality the solution of the main questions facing industrial civilization at the present time is impossible. As we have seen, this problem of personality cannot be solved, cannot even be properly stated, until we have found, through reflection upon our knowledge of the personal in immediate experience, the unity-pattern within which the expression of that knowledge could be achieved. The primary problem is a problem of logic.

The traditional logic in any of its forms is inadequate to undertake this task. It is based upon the study of those forms of reflection which arise in connexion with our immediate experience either of matter or of organic life. In these fields, as we have seen, the thinker can stand over against the world about which he reflects. It is possible, therefore, to conceive a pure thought which is unaffected by its object and independent of its object. But when personality itself is the object of thought this is no longer possible. The thinker himself as a person is part of what he thinks about, and his thinking is itself part of him. Thought is now one of the functions of the object of thought. It is not even logically prior to its object. Pure thought—that is to say, thought which may be taken for practical purposes as independent of the other functions of personality because it is concerned with what does not include

## LOGIC AND LIFE

personality—is no longer possible. We reach the point at which psychology and logic interpenetrate. We are forced to recognize that all thought is psychologically conditioned.

To say that thought is psychologically conditioned is to say that it is socially conditioned, since human nature is essentially social. Thought, therefore, is never the activity of an artificially isolated individual. The individual thinker is necessarily the member of a particular community at a particular point in the development of history. His thinking is historically conditioned because it is socially conditioned. All thought is in a very real sense communal thought. The individual's thinking is one aspect of his activity as a person. He cannot lift himself out of his place in the historic process of human society and become a pure consciousness. He cannot, by any miracle of levitation, suspend himself in vacuity above the process of world-history and look down upon it from outside. His thinking is part of the history upon which he reflects.

It is often argued by philosophers that if this is true, knowledge is impossible. Such a view brings the process of thought within the stream of determinism. The conclusions of all thinking must then be determined, not in terms of truth, but in terms of psychological pressure. What I believe, I believe merely because I am the kind of person I am. That in its turn is determined by heredity and environment, over which I have no control. There is no need to undertake the refutation of this argument. It is one of the results of thinking within the unity-pattern of organic symbolism, and within that unity-pattern it is logically unassailable. But to describe the nature of personality in organic terms is to misrepresent it and so to vitiate all conclusions which refer to reality in so far as it is personal. This particular argument rests upon the implicit assumption that all knowledge is a function of reflective thought, and that thought, therefore, is logically prior to knowledge. This assumption is not merely ungrounded, it is palpably untrue. Knowledge is prior to thought, for thought can only be about what is known. This primary knowledge is, as we have seen, an aspect of the complete, concrete life of personal activity

## LOGIC AND LIFE

and has its own development which is not dependent, in essence, upon the activity of reflective thought. Once this is realized, the difficulty vanishes. We can test and check the results of thinking by that knowledge which is our consciousness *in* the historic process of social development.

The proper conclusion to be drawn from the recognition that all thought is psychologically conditioned is not that thought cannot be trusted, but that its trustworthiness depends upon the trustworthiness of the person in whose consciousness it goes on. At the point where reflection becomes reflection upon personality, it becomes itself part of a developing reality. Its failure becomes a failure to remain completely in touch with and subordinate to the process of reality. Under such conditions, thought becomes unreal, because its function in the process of personal experience is denied or perverted. It becomes isolated within personality. However free it may be from internal or theoretical contradictions, there is a practical contradiction at its roots. At every point it is liable to be in contradiction with the practical activity and, therefore, with the emotional life which is the source of practical activity, of the individual whose thought it is. Such thinking may, indeed, be true, but there is no real reason to expect that it will be true, or that the arguments used to support it, however cogent they may appear, are worth consideration. Thought divorced from life is inherently unreal and untrustworthy. Common sense is thoroughly justified in distrusting the conclusions of thinkers when they are contradicted by their practice, or who reveal an emotional insincerity as the background of their theorizing.

Since thinking is an activity, it must, like all activities, have a motive, and all motives are emotional. When a man says that he thinks for the sake of thinking, he is either displaying an ignorance of his real motives or he is proclaiming himself the devotee of the most meagre and unsubstantial of all the forms of hedonism. The best cure for hedonism is the attempt to practice it; but, unfortunately, when hedonism takes to the field of the imagination and exerts itself in the unreal activities of reflection, there is

## LOGIC AND LIFE

no cure, because it refuses to verify itself in life. Most thinking, however, is determined by motives which are hidden even from the thinker. All serious thought which professes to be governed by the pure love of truth is of this kind. Theory and practice are bound together in the nature of things, and the bond is a common motive. If thought, then, is to be real and function as it should in the unity of personal life, it must be carried on in full awareness of the conditions which determine it. The sense of freedom in thinking which arises from ignoring the psychological conditions in which alone it is possible, is spurious. True freedom, Hegel said, is the consciousness of necessity. It is at least true that the sense of freedom which arises from the ignorance of necessity can be nothing but a deception. If thought is psychologically conditioned, the only possible way to reach a real understanding by means of thought must be to become fully aware of the conditions under which our thinking is carried on. For this reason, our philosophizing, if it is to have any value, must rest upon the psychological understanding of personality. The development of a scientific psychology is perhaps the most urgent need of our time, both in the theoretical and in the practical field. This does not mean that the philosopher must accept the theories of modern psychology and base his own thought upon them. Such a view would be completely contrary to everything that has been urged in this book. Modern psychology fails, in the theoretical field, because the type of thinking which could express the nature of personality, the type of analysis which the psychological enquiry demands, is not available. It is the business of philosophy to supply it. On the other hand, the researches of psychologists, particularly in the field of medical psychology where theory is necessarily controlled by personal fact, force upon us, in a way that nothing else can, the empirical problems for which an adequate instrument of analysis is demanded. They also reveal and crystallize into definite form the difficulties of applying either the mathematical or the organic conception for the elucidation of the known facts. It is in the combination of a rich knowledge of the personal field in immediate experience with the study of

## LOGIC AND LIFE

modern psychology that the hope of discovering the unity-pattern of personal thought most probably lies. In the field of psychology, however, we must include all such systematic efforts as are made to bring into consciousness the psychological factors in human life, whether in the study of society, of history or of the individual. One of our first needs is for an effort to interpret the development of history, particularly of European history, from the psychological point of view, as a history of the development of consciousness. It is in that field that the development of thought can be most easily recognized as part of the development of immediate experience. For it is in the historic process of human development that life and logic interpenetrate, and that philosophy is continuously, if unconsciously, submitted to the processes of verification.

# Index

Absolute, personal, 78
Abstraction, process of, 22
— of science, 57
Action, primariness of, 19–20
Activity, real and reflective, 10, 20, 90–11; spontaneous, 9, 75; practical, 45, 82, 90; symbolic, 42, 47, 51
Algebra, 37–38
Analysis, arbitrariness of, 28; mathematical, 51, 58; descriptive, 28
Apprehension, of matter, 59, 60ff; of life, 67
Art, 62, 76, 77

Bergson, 57
Berkeley, 55
Biological thought, limitations of, 65; unity-pattern of, 58ff, 65, 67; inadequacy of, 68; problem of, 83; development of, 85
Biology, 66ff

Cartesians, 69
Causality, and change, 53; problem of, 53; and causal properties, 49ff
Cause, 49ff, 56
Certainty, 43
Change, 53ff, 60

Civilization, 82, 88
Cognition, 18
Conclusions, verification of, 41; guarantee of, 41
Consciousness, content of, 74; human, 68; of ourselves, 71; subjective, objective, 72–73, 74, 78; personal, 74
Common sense, 1, 11, 22, 44, 90

Data, 29
Determinism, 54, 55–56
Development, idea of, 63ff; 85
Differences, of function, 65; harmony of, 65; unity of, 67ff
Doubt, 19
Dreams, 73
Dualism of matter and mind, 57

Effect, 49ff, 56
Emotions, 75
Enmity, 76
Environment, 74; adaptation to, 85; control of, 82, 83ff, 86–87; and finite organisms, 68
Error, problem of, 36
— in description, 37
— in conclusion, 37
— in judgment, 75
— and subjectivity, 77
Existence, 11

# INDEX

Experience, conscious, 74; subject of, 78
Experiment, 42ff, 51
Expression, result of thought, 25; symbolic, 37, 38–39

Feeling, 60, 62, 75
Finite, unreality of, 16
Freedom, 91
Friendship, 76ff

Generalization, 39ff
God, 70, 78
Growth, 60, 61, 62, 63ff, 85
*Gulliver's Travels*, 45

Hallucinations, 15
Hedonism, 90
Hegel, 46, 65, 91
History, 45, 82, 83, 84, 92
Hume, 15, 45

Idealism, modern, 65, 67
Ideas, private symbols, 25; unreality of, 16–17
Imagery, reduction of, 22
Images, and things, distinction of, 20; abstract, 23; reduced, 24; manipulation of, 35, 36; elementary and composite, 36
Imagination, activity of, 29, 30–31; process of, 35; spontaneity of, 39
Immediate experience, definition of, 4, 8, 9–10; characteristic of, 12–14; of persons, 69, 70; and sense-perception, 14–15; and thought, 92
Incarnation, 70
Individuality, 79, 79–80
Industrialism, 85ff, 90
Infinite, 16, 38; apprehension of, 70

— factor, 38–39
Intellect, 57
Intellectualism, definition of, 11

Judgment, 29–37; false, 75; and inference, 27

Kant, 32, 55, 69
Knowledge, 6, 9, 17; definition of, 7; and certainty, 43; and thought, 35, 82; immediate, 6; scientific, 6; of persons, 78; possibility of, 89; priority of, 81–82, 89–90; theory of knowledge, 81; problem of, 11

Language, symbolism of, 24; function of, 24ff
Life, definition of, 18; knowledge of, 59–60; material basis of, 61; and logic, 82, 92; subordination of, 87; social control of, 87–88; emotional, 90
Logic, and irrationality, 19; and spontaneity of the mind, 30; justification of, 82; primary social problem, 88; inadequacy of, 88

Materialism, 55ff
Mathematical thought, methods, 84; limitations of, 38, 54–55; symbolism of, 39, 52, 54; postulate of, 51; irrationality of, 51–52; and science, 55, 57; unity-pattern of, 48ff, 61, 80
Matter, 53, 56, 60ff, 86
Means and ends, 49
Mechanism, 54, 66, 85–86

Newton, 84

# INDEX

Objectivity, 72–73, 74ff, 77
Organism, conception of, 65

Patterns, basic, 33; unity-patterns, 32–33; of mathematics, 50
Percept and symbol, 23
Personality, immediate knowledge of, 59; unity of, 70; essential nature of, 70, 75, 88, 89; key to the nature of, 76; and self-consciousness, 77–78
Philosophy, definition of, 3, 16ff; conception of, 1–2; central problem of, 80, 81; task of, 2, 3; and science, 6, 12; verification of, 45, 92; and experiment, 45–46; and mathematical thought, 55–56; and biological thought, 68
Potentiality, 64, 65
Psychology, 69; problem of, 83; and logic, 89; failure of, 91
Purpose, 64

Qualitative infinity of universe, 12

Rationality, 72, 74–75, 75–76, 76ff, 81
Realism, modern, 65, 67
Reality, 12, 16–17, 28, 40, 41, 47–48, 50–51, 52, 54, 70, 72, 90
Reason, 74
Reflection, 3, 8, 9–10; philosophical, 11; cause of, 18; interruption of living, 19, 20; unreality of, 48, 49, 70, 81, 90
Reflective thought, problem of, 79; unity-pattern of, 70; activity of, 27ff
Religion, 77

Renaissance, 83
Russia, 45

Schopenhauer, 60
Science, and philosophy, 6, 12; and theory, 43; thought and action, 44; and mathematical thought, 55, 57, 85; emergence of, 83; development of, 83, 84
Self, 13, 71, 78
Sense-data, 15
Sense-perception, 14–15, 41, 60
Social problem, 85, 87–88
Space, 16, 52, 54
Space-time, 14, 16
Spinoza, 16, 55
St. Paul, 78
Subjectivity, 73, 74, 76
Supposal, 30, 31ff
Symbols, production of, 23, 39; definition of, 26; pattern of, 28; manipulation of, 37–38, 40

Teleology, 63, 64; limitation of, 67
Theory, and immediate experience, 44; and practice, 91
Thinking, definition of, 3, 29; and imagination, 36; generalization in, 39; anthropomorphic, 59; rational, 72
Thought, 10–11, 19, 47; origin of, 42; abnormal, 19; secondary, 19; activities of, 29, 33; unreality of, 20, 90; and immediate experience, 35; conclusions of, 41; rationality of, 74–75; and sense-perception, 41; pure, 88
Time, 52
Truth, guarantee of, 40, 42–43; problem of, 36; love of, 91

# INDEX

Unit, entities, 37; elements, 53, 55

Unity, structural, 32, 47; of immediate experience; 47, 70; of growth, 61; of differences, 62ff; organic, 62; of personality, 70; of persons, 78

Unity-pattern, 32–33; mechanical, 48ff, 61; organic, 58ff, 66–67, 76, 89; of reflective thought, 70, 80; personal, 77

Universe, definition of, 12, 56, 68

Unreal, definition of, 52

Utopia, 87

Value, 48

Verification, necessity of, 41; experimental, 43, 44; of scientific conclusion, 44

Vitalism, 66

Voltaire, 45

World, reduced image, 24ff; primary function, 26